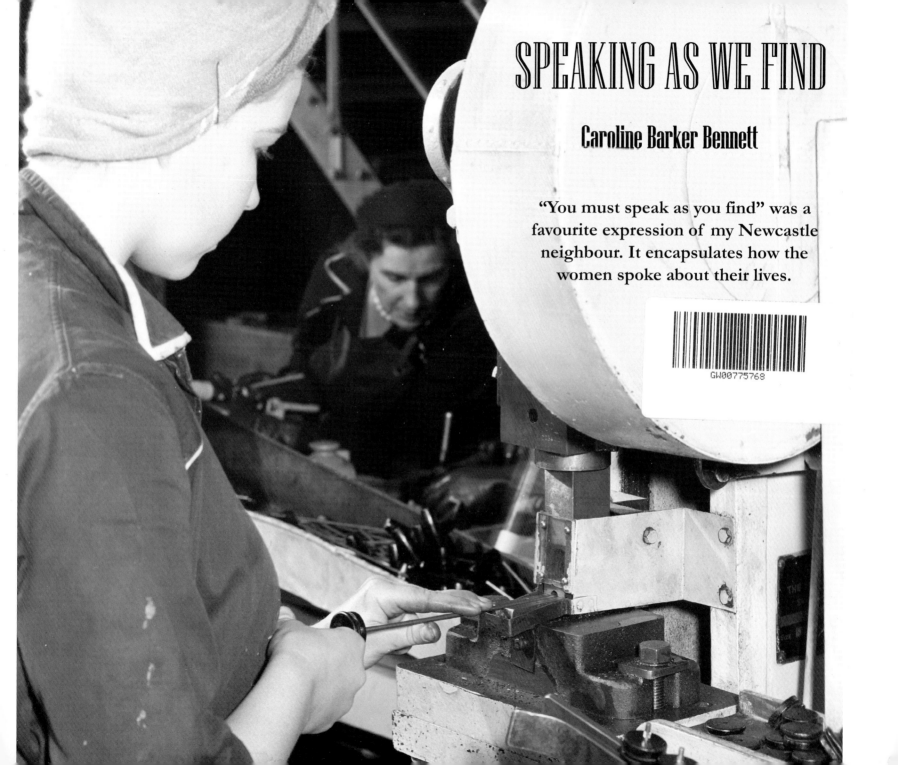

SPEAKING AS WE FIND

Caroline Barker Bennett

"You must speak as you find" was a favourite expression of my Newcastle neighbour. It encapsulates how the women spoke about their lives.

Published by:

City of Newcastle Upon Tyne

Newcastle Libraries

Tyne Bridge Publishing, 2023

unless otherwise indicated

The photographs in this book are the copyright of Newcastle Library Service
unless otherwise stated

All names of participants in this book, and those referred to, have been changed

Photos: Previous page: A worker at the Metal Box Company, Heaton, 1956. Opposite page: Coop Dairy Equipment Works in Wingate, 1951. Front Cover: Women working at the John Sinclair tobacco factory in Bath Lane, Newcastle, 1949.

CONTENTS

FOREWORD

It is an honour to write the foreword to this book. It brings to life a period in which industrial life in the north east and the role of women within it grew enormously. Now women across the north east are at the forefront of the trade union movement, working to gain improvements in the working lives of the people of the region. Through the vivid accounts of the women, who describe their experience of working in shops, factories and other workplaces, we see how these developments began. We move from the North Shields Fish Quay in the 1930s, when life was extremely tough, to an account of how women set up their own clothing cooperative in Hebburn in the 1980s. I was struck by the warmth of these stories and how they depict a deep trust between the author and the women, our sisters in struggle.

It is important to highlight the importance of the book's themes today: the story of increasing and declining union power in core north east industries; the impact of automation on jobs and livelihoods; poor management practice; the struggle women have to be valued in their workplaces and unions. These struggles continue. Forty years after the interviews the issues resonate: the high cost of living and the prevalence of casual and minimum wage-based employment in the region still cause suffering.

The importance of trade union education available at the time, highlighted in the book, continues today and is critical to our success as unions as we fight for union recognition and improvements to pay, terms and conditions.

It is heartening to witness the character and power of the north east in these stories and recollections. Then as now they are resilient, dignified, humorous and rooted in solidarity. Thank you, Caroline and all the sisters in this book, who show us how our proud history continues to educate and support workers today and tomorrow.

Liz Blackshaw,
Regional Secretary, Northern TUC

ACKNOWLEDGEMENTS

This book is dedicated to the women who contributed to it; who made me welcome when I arrived from the south and were willing to share the stories of their working lives with me.

My thanks to: Derek Tree of Tyne Bridge Publishing, who saw value in the book and took on the editing; to Dr Bill Williamson who started me on the project and supervised my thesis; to Liz Blackshaw of the NTUC for writing the foreword. I would also like to thank Martin Stott for allow us to use his photographs of the Louise Argyle factory.

About the author

Caroline Barker Bennett was born in Limpsfield, Surrey in 1944. She read English at New Hall, Cambridge, and then taught English for four years before, first, running a youth and community centre in Clapham and then working for a youth project in rural Surrey.

She became a Lay Reader in Southwark Diocese in 1976 and moved to Newcastle Diocese in 1977 to be an industrial chaplain. In 1990, she moved to Manchester to be the Director of Education for the Diocese. Her final job was in the same role for Bristol Diocese. She now shares a house with her sister beside the River Wylye in Wiltshire.

Photo Credit: Barnabas Wilson.

Members of the Louise Argyle Co-operative, in Hebburn, c1982.

Photo Credit: Martin Stott.

INTRODUCTION

This book takes us back to the beginning of the 1980s: the Thatcher government was in power and the Miners' Strike was brewing. It is written to tell something of the story of women industrial workers on Tyneside and is based on recorded conversations with twenty women: the eldest started work in 1934 and the youngest in 1981.

These recordings were made in the winter of 1983 - 84 and were the basis of a research degree with the Department of Sociology & Social Policy at Durham University. They arose from my work as an industrial chaplain. I got to know the women through visiting George Angus, an engineering company in Wallsend, and Louise Argyle, a women's clothing co-operative, in Hebburn.

In the first place I was struck by the vividness of their recollections and moved by the hardships they described which they took for granted. It was only gradually that I realised that these personal stories give an account of the history of women's employment in the region during the period: working on the Fish Quay at North Shields in the 1930s; working in shops and factories post-war; running the shop at the Rising Sun pit in Wallsend; setting up Louise Argyle, a women's clothing co-operative in Hebburn, in the 1980s.

I have now re-written the material, leaving out the academic references which made it a thesis and concentrating on what the women said. While this makes for lighter reading, it is not a popular "tales of canny Tyneside women" but a serious account of women's employment. My aim originally was to explore with the women, whom I mostly knew well, what had been their experience as workers since leaving school: what different kinds of job they had done; what kinds of responsibilities they had held at work and how these had combined with their responsibilities at home.

The two workplaces were interesting for particular reasons: George Angus was an engineering works where women worked alongside men and were represented jointly with them by the General & Municipal Workers Union - women were more usually employed in all-female workplaces where the power of trade unions was weak; the women at Louise Argyle were running their own business. Behind these particular features were the traditions and culture of the north east of England.

The popular Andy Capp image of the north east is of a culture of male chauvinism, derived from the heavy industry and mining upon which the region depended from its nineteenth century beginnings. Traditionally women were seen as those who looked after the men, enabling them to do the heavy work their jobs demanded. While to outward appearances the men were the powerful figures, in practice the women were lynch pins of family and society, exercising financial control of their households and having charge of the upbringing of children.

As we shall hear, mothers were key figures in influencing their daughters' choices of jobs on leaving school; they were advisers when the women took on new roles as wives, mothers and even shop stewards. In several of these accounts, mothers come over as more important figures than husbands.

Invisibility of Women Industrial Workers in the North East

When I set out to discover published material about women workers in the north east, in order to put the oral material in a wider context, I found a problem. It was very difficult to find anything written on the subject. On the other hand, I was continually referred to people who would be glad to tell me of their experience. One man told me of a neighbour who had vivid memories of working at Vickers during the war; another, who had been an apprentice at Vickers in the thirties, had heard the screams of a woman whose hair had got caught in machinery. He had been afraid to tell his mother in case she thought he worked in a very rough place.

When I asked a woman librarian where I might find material and said that I was beginning to feel that women were invisible, she said, "Oh they are," and immediately started to tell me about her own experience.

Workers at Benwell Resource Centre, who were trying to mount an exhibition about Women & Work, told me they had had the same frustrating experience but had also been referred to mothers and grandmothers who could give graphic accounts of industrial jobs.

I tried company magazines but found that women were only mentioned when getting married, having a baby, or retiring. In fairness, the work of shop floor male workers is not much documented either. This makes what the women I talked to said about their experience very valuable. They bring to life their working lives and the cultures of the various workplaces to which they belonged. "You must speak as you find" was a favourite expression of my Newcastle neighbour. It encapsulates how the women spoke about their lives.

Caroline Barker Bennett in the Tool Room at George Angus in 1981

Introducing The Women Whose Stories We Hear

The chapters which follow are arranged chronologically and compare the women's experiences from leaving school onwards. We therefore hear snippets of their lives rather than anyone's story as a whole. To help the reader to keep track of who is who, here are brief biographies of the main speakers.

Those born in the 1920s, who started work before the Second World War included: **Phyllis**, **Vera** and **Margaret**. Because **Vera's** life exemplified so much about the lives of women industrial workers on Tyneside in the period, I give her story as a whole after the briefer accounts of all the others.

Phyllis left school in 1934 aged 14. She lived in North Shields and started her working life as a domestic servant in Tynemouth on a wage of four shillings a week. She found the life very hard and ran away twice, only to be brought back by her mother. When she managed to leave she worked in a cafe until the war came which brought her a job on the railways, first as a dining-car attendant and then as a station hand. She volunteered for the army where she learned to drive lorries. At the end of the war, she got a job driving a bread van before becoming a supervisor in a sweet factory. After a confrontation with the management, she moved to Angus's.

Margaret came from a large Roman Catholic family. She left school in 1940. She had vivid memories of her first job working, along with the rest of her family, at Maling's famous Tyneside pottery. They made, as she said, "everything from something that goes under the bed to something that goes on the wall".

Seeing a recruiting film for the Land Army made her determined to join. She had a struggle to get Maling's to sign the form, "By heavens, they wouldn't let me out of that Maling's pottery". But she persisted. "I just thought joining the Land Army was a way of seeing new worlds". She was right about this. In many ways her experience was similar to that of a student going away to college. She learned to drive a lorry and after the war would have gone as a driver to Wimpey's, the building firm, had she not got drawn into a temporary job at Angus's. The machinery interested her and the family network drew her in as it had at Maling's. So she stayed at Angus's for thirty years, nearly all as a supervisor.

Alice and **June** were a little younger and started work as the war was ending. They were destined to become, in 1981, founding members of Louise Argyle, the workers' clothing co-operative in Hebburn.

June worked as a machinist for most of her life, starting in the great Co-op factories at Pelaw. She remembered that there were still "these cross-legged tailors - 'tinker tailors' we used to call them - used to sit cross-legged and they'd edge-stitch round - in fact they'd made suits without any machining, all hand done."

Over the years she saw the introduction of different piecework systems and more sophisticated machinery. Bringing up her family, largely on her own, she found that being a machinist was a useful skill always in demand.

Alice enjoyed sewing and making things at school and wanted to use these skills in a job. But her parents felt she could do better in an office job. She went into the Ministry of National Insurance but, as she said, "I got my own way at the finish" and moved to the dressmaking workrooms at Binns' department store. From there she moved to a handbag factory where she worked till she got married. It was only eighteen years later, when her children were growing up, that she determined to break out of her domestic role and got a job as a machinist.

Five of the women started work in the 1950s. Of these, only **Nancy**, who went into clothing, did not start in shop work. Their mothers encouraged them, feeling that shop work was nice work for a girl.

Jeanette described how she was left with great financial responsibility in the high-class grocer's where she worked as a very young woman and how rudely she was treated by the manager of a Co-op store she worked in. It was only when she accompanied her sister to an interview at Osram's that she got over her prejudice about working in factories and took a job there as well. Faced with bringing up her daughter as a single parent, **Jeanette** took jobs in other factories without telling them that she had a child for fear they would not employ her. After many years of struggle she became a shop steward and, through her union's education programme, found an outlet for the talents which would have been apparent, if anyone had been interested, when she worked in the grocer's.

Audrey's working life followed a similar pattern to **Jeanette's**. She began working in shops and moved into factory work for better wages when she was getting married. A special experience was helping her mother run the colliery shop at the Rising Sun pit before the pit closed. Her experience there is described in the chapter on "A Way of Life That Went".

When she went back to working at Angus's after this interlude, **Audrey** took on several shop floor responsibilities for training, health & safety and work-study. Nevertheless **Audrey** still felt that it was up to her to have the dinner for her husband and son on the table for 4.45pm. If her job had interfered with her home commitments, she said, she would have given it up. Sadly, what compelled her to give up work prematurely, was back trouble brought on by lifting at work.

Brenda worked at Angus's from 1959. She went there after a year working in a Co-op greengrocery. Her bid for a career with training in the police or prison service was prevented: partly because she wore glasses, but also because her mother was afraid she would be "punched around and badly used".

Her reflections on her long experience of working at Angus's in different jobs, as a shop steward and as Assistant Convener, were very valuable to me in writing about Angus's. Like Jeanette, she benefited greatly from her union's education programme. This gave her knowledge and confidence on which to draw in her work with management and members.

Nancy went straight into the clothing industry when she left school in 1958. Her mother felt it was a career she "could always fall back on". She found, like **June**, that her skills as a machinist were constantly in demand. Although **Nancy** had the support of a working husband, she found herself wanting to go back to work rather than staying at home full-time. She described how many practical and subtle difficulties there were to be overcome in making this possible including her children's needs, her husband's reactions and her own feelings of guilt. Managing all these responsibilities **Nancy** described as, "with us rushing all the time it's hard to unwind and slow down. Even when I'm busy doing my housework I think I'm on piecework!"

Those who started work in the sixties and early seventies: **Julie**, **Rachel**, **Sally** and **Yvonne**, varied little in their experience from those in preceding generations. **Julie**, who worked in clothing from leaving school, had much the same experience as **June** and **Nancy**. Later on, her part-time work in a club gave her useful management experience for her role at Louise Argyle.

Rachel went straight to Angus's and stayed there until she took voluntary redundancy, hoping to start a family. **Sally** appeared to be in a good position as a member of a printing union while still at school and therefore assured of well-paid employment. She, however, rebelled against being thus pigeon-holed. She tried many different printing jobs; moved away from Tyneside and worked in a crisp factory; eventually returned and settled in to working at Angus's where first the piecework system and then working on the permanent night shift appealed to her.

Yvonne started work in a very different world from that of Tyneside industry - a hunting stable in the Borders. Her experience in that aristocratic world seemed akin to the 1934 world of Phyllis in domestic service. The difference was that, while Phyllis hated it and ran away, Yvonne loved it and would have stayed except that finding permanent work with horses was difficult. Marriage, as for others of the women, meant for her a job in a factory.

A job in a factory, despised by those in older generations, was a sought-after thing for those who found themselves as school leavers at the end of the seventies and early eighties. **Pam** and **Pat** went into jobs in clothing and worked as juniors at Louise Argyle. **Jane**, whom I met briefly at Angus's in the summer of 1984, had to take badly paid jobs in fast-food businesses working unsocial hours. After fruitlessly applying to many factories, she heard from a neighbours' network that there might be a job at Angus's. Having applied in January, she was eventually contacted in May. She said that since coming to Angus's she "felt employable again". Her husband was not so lucky. Having been made redundant from his job as a labourer in engineering, he had been out of work for three years with little prospect of finding a job. I asked if he felt bad about being dependent on **Jane**. "He doesn't say anything but I know he does, especially since I started here".

We begin with hearing the life story of **Vera**. It included in full because, while **Vera's** is the personal story of a particular woman, her life mirrored much that was taking place in women's employment on Tyneside between 1935 and 1980 as a result of social developments and government initiatives. She was born in North Shields in 1921.

Vera's Story

"When I was a girl, I lived at the Fish Quay end of the town. Me mother worked in the kippering - that was the yards where you make the kippers. Well, before I left school, when I used to finish school at four o'clock, naturally I used to go round to the yard where me mam worked and I got to see how the women were making kippers. So, being inquisitive, I started having a little go. Well, in those days the only thing that there was in this town was either the Fish Quay, "the smoke house" as we called it, Hutton Haggies [the Rope Works], which was out, and Tyne Brand. I had no fancy for Tyne Brand - or service. No, service was a thing I had never ever gone for because it... I'm not house minded - to a point. So it was the Fish Quay. So I decided that was it. So I left school on the Friday at 4pm and got started the Saturday morning, on the Fish Quay."

The Fish Quay

"In those days you went in as a learner which was, you had to do all the menial tasks, all the humping and carrying, and then you got to handle the herring themselves. They bring the herring in and they're loaded up onto benches, split open, the innards removed. Then they're put onto what they call a tenter stick and it's a stick with a series of hooks on to which you hook the herring, back to the wood. Then they're taken and they're hung in what they call kilns, "houses" as we used to call them. They're smoked more or less overnight. They're brought out of a morning and they have to be packed in boxes.''

"Well, then, I started at 14 as what they called a "twopence halfpenny learner". Now that was, you got twopence halfpenny an hour for your work. Now you only worked when the work was there. You weren't on a set wage. You only got paid by the hour, so it meant 'No work, no money'. Well, in those days, dole, that was also only a pittance but if you worked one hour of that day you couldn't claim dole for that day. Your one hour had to suffice. Failing that, if there was no herring in, you went and you signed the dole, for which you got a day's dole. But there was a snag to that as well because you had to have three clear days before you got anything. So, the way it worked out it was pathetic really. I

Women working at the North Shields Fish Quay in the 1930s.

up. Really it was hard going. But, having said that, the type of women that worked there were a jovial lot, and it didn't matter when you passed the yard, you could hear the women singing."

"As you progressed through this work you got to be from a twopence-halfpenny learner - your wage was increased by a halfpenny an hour according to how you picked the job up. The more experience you got - if your boss was good he would give you another halfpenny an hour. But we discovered, once we had a little bit of experience, it was more beneficial to try for a job somewhere else and you'd go as a halfpenny an hour more. Because you were sick of waiting for this fellow giving it you, you know! And you worked up till you were a fourpence an hour learner. Oh, you were doing very well! And then you graduated - the full money was sevenpence an hour in old money. Now that was the highest money you could get. So it was trying to get into a yard that could get plenty of work and you were all right."

Vera went on to describe how hard the life was: "There was an awful lot of hardship to the point where women were pregnant, married women. Now I've worked in a yard where a woman was standing working. She's taken her labour, the boss has had to put her on the lorry, take her home. Within a few hours that woman has had her baby. Within a few hours, we'll say a day, that woman has been back working because times were such in those days - no work, no money. The baby was brought to work with her in the pram and it used to be a communal pram. The one pram used to be passed from one, you know, if somebody was pregnant: 'Keep on to your pram!' And the pram was brought and, mind, if you had a good boss he would let the pram stand in the office to keep the baby reasonably warm. And the mother,

mean you'd go to the dole and you'd come away with maybe's a shilling, as the money was in those days. You got paid when you finished on a Saturday. Now that pay, it was whatever time you finished on a Saturday. Now it always seemed to be in those days (whether it was the boats wanted to be in for the weekend) - but most of the herring boats used to come in on a Saturday. And I've worked from Saturday morning six o'clock start (and you must work the herring up that the boss has bought), and I've seen me two or three o'clock in the morning when we've been coming away from that Fish Quay because the herring must be worked when the baby needed feeding, she used to have to go and wash her hands, remove her oilskins, sit and feed her baby and there it went on."

"I mean there's nothing that can compare with the Fish Quay. The environment that you worked in. You stood in yards where, because of the nature of your work, the heating was limited, so it was a very, very cold place to work in, which has been in a way bad. You had to wear rubber boots all day. Nearly all the women that have worked there have ended up with varicose veins and all this type of thing, with working with the frozen fish. It affected people, a lot of people, with rheumatics and that sort of thing."

There were more light-hearted moments. Her story of *Gone with the Wind* shows how parochial the world of North Shields was, how overriding were the demands of the fishing industry and how you could not go to the cinema without its being known! There seems to have been no boundary between work and leisure hours.

Vera told the story: "The Prince's Cinema (it's the Crown Bingo now) we used to love if we could possibly make it on a Monday all the girls used to go to the matinee. Actually, at first it used to be a little bit of a dodge. Well, if they came for us for work - we're at the pictures. The firm cottoned on, and one day, I'll never forget it. We were at *Gone with the Wind* and it came up on the screen - all our names! And we had to report to the front foyer and when we went it was the boss who was standing there and he says, 'Come on, the lot of you'. Apparently, a boat had come in with an exceptional load of herring. We had to go home, change and go down and work. I'll never forget that because we worked from about, what, three o'clock in the afternoon by the time we got home, got changed, on to the Fish Quay. We worked till about 4 am. We worked right through.

Now the thing was, it didn't matter how late you finished in the early morning, you still had to turn out again for 6 o'clock. And I always remember - I came home - 'course me mother was worried about how late I was and that - came home and the boss was a little bit lenient and he says, "Well, don't come back until 7am under the circumstances.' We had about four hours and I knew that to go to bed would be fatal. So me mam give me me breakfast, got me on the settee, and back to work again. But somehow once you got to work you thought nothing of that sort of thing. The only thing that peeved us was that it was *Gone with*

the Wind! We made a pact with the boss. Of course, we all ranted at him for having done this to us. He says, 'I'll tell you what I'll do. Seeing that you girls were so good to do this for me, I'll let you take your turns, and I'll pay for you and you can go back and see *Gone with the Wind'*. Because I think it was on for two or three weeks. And that was the way we got over the thing."

The "Travelling Shop"

Vera was fortunate in getting a job in a "travelling shop" and so she extricated herself from the uncertainties of the work on the Fish Quay: "Now they had some yards, the bigger firms, they had smoke houses in different parts of the country and it was easier to take these women and men to that yard than to bring the herring up the road. So you tried to get into what we called a "travelling shop", which was a one where you used to travel.

"Now I was in Great Yarmouth, Hull, Grimsby - as the herring moved around the coast so you moved with it, you see. Now the beauty of that job, you were on a set wage. Actually I was in Gourock working the day that war broke out and I was then on a wage of 30/- per week, which was a great thing. Because you got that 30/- whether you worked or not. You had to have that 30/-, and as long as the herring were there you worked there. And of course as they moved on again you'd go from Gourock to Mallaig. So, as well as having this job you were seeing a little bit of the country.

"We used to go into digs. More often than not there used to be four girls - either two or four. We used to have what we called a "housey purse". Now we used to each put six shillings a week in the housey purse and six shillings a week each to the landlady for the room. If you had a nice canny landlady, if you bought your food she would cook it for you coming in. But if you had an indifferent landlady, well, you had to run in on a dinner time, do something and then evenings for your evening meal. But the point was you finished at 6pm. You never worked over 6pm unless there was overtime, which was beneficial. But that was very, very rare that you got overtime because the way the herring used to come in you could normally work - you had enough work to keep you going from six in the morning till six at night.

"Now Mallaig. When we used to go to Mallaig, there they only had one train a day to take the herring out of Mallaig. It came in by sea by the herring boats. It went out by train because then there was no way of getting into Mallaig other than by the train or by the sea. You couldn't go out by car because they hadn't advanced with their roadways in those days, you know. So we had to start work there at five o'clock in the morning.

"Now while we lived in Mallaig we lived in... they were like a type of hut. They had the old-fashioned galley stoves so it meant if you were starting work at five o'clock in the morning, you took your turn of getting up, you had to light this fire before you got a cup of tea. Because there was no electricity in these huts, they were all paraffin lamps. Now that made that a hard job in that respect, but on the other hand you were working with girls who were a happy lot. When you worked away in those travel shops you see, more so in Scotland, the herring boats never go out on a Sunday night. So on a Monday morning you'd go in and you'd pack up the kippers that you had done on Saturday. You used to start work at 6am. Well, by about 9am they were all packed up and on the waggons and on their way so the rest of the day was your day off to explore.

"What you sort of lost on the swings you gained on the roundabouts, because it was a happy environment plus the fact that you had a job, that was the thing. When we used to go to Mallaig there wasn't anything. There were no picture halls, nothing. There were two public houses which we couldn't afford to go into really. But to compensate that, one of the lads that worked with us, he had one of these small accordions. There was a small farm near us in Mallaig and they had a barn and on Saturday nights we used to go up, and the lads used to clean the barn out and we used to have the greatest dance there. Mind, everybody that worked in the yards used to go there and you used to have a great night. But we could even just go on the wharf when we finished at night and the lad used to come with his accordion and that made up.

In fact in those days you didn't need a lot to entertain you. Plus, the fact that we used to rise at about four o'clock in the morning. If we could get a couple of hours up there it used to be great. It was hard but it was satisfying. But at the time that you're working it, you never think about it. It wasn't till later years when I left it and went into the factories, then the comparison came in."

Vera's description of her life before the war emphasises the huge importance that having any kind of regular job represented for people on Tyneside in the thirties. It also reflects the cheerful solidarity in adversity and the communal nature of working class life in the north east at that time.

The War

When the war came, Vera was not fit for military service because she had been, as she said, "hospitalised for a while with a T.B. abdomen". Since she was apparently clear of the disease she was regarded as fit enough to work in munitions.

"Well, we were working at Gourock so four of us managed to get into munitions. The rest had to go into Services, and they kept only the older women for to work in the yards. That was a little bit of an essential because it was foodstuff. I went to work in the Greenock torpedo factory, which suited me because I loved that part of the country."

"We lived there in hostels. Well then the wage rose to, oh, I would say about £2.15s a week, which was a good thing. That was a start, and of course as the war advanced it was risen a bit because you had unions and one thing and another then. And the money gradually rose, not a lot, but enough to meet your needs. I was there until the war finished. Now in there, it was more or less work like Angus's, something similar, making caps for shells. But it was more or less capstan work, power presses. And I worked there till the war finished."

Greenock torpedo factory.

Vera's experience of war work in factories reflects the improvements brought about in wages and conditions, partly as a result of trade union pressure and partly because of the work of industrial welfare officers and government initiatives. These movements for change were successful because of the desperate need for armaments and other supplies for the war effort and the shortage of labour to produce these. These improvements continued in the period after the war.

Working in Factories

Vera, looking back over her experience, said: "I worked from 14, and I started in the factories when I was 21. Things were so much easier in the factories. When I first went in the factories you started at 7.30am and your finishing time was 5.30pm. Now that whittled down to 7.30am to 4pm. Well, that made an awful big difference on your day.

"When you worked in factories you had proper toilet facilities, which were a good thing; you had proper tea breaks, which was something we'd never had on the Fish Quay. [There] you started at six in the morning. You got half an hour break for your breakfast. To break again before dinner time, before twelve o'clock, was unheard of. But on an odd time, if it was exceptionally cold, the boss would let someone make a cup of tea. But you had to have it standing, so you can imagine - a mug of tea in among the herring - and you were having your filthy hands. But when you went into the factory you had your hands washed and you sat down and you had your cup of tea and your cigarette. Oh, things changed enormously!

"And you started to have a little bit more say in factories. If you didn't like the way the foreman was treating you or something like that, you could go and complain either to management or union and something was done about it. But prior to that, in the Fish Quay, if you had a complaint to the boss he would say, 'Right, you're finished' and there was nothing you could do about it - you were finished".

After the War

At the end of the war, Vera returned to Tyneside: "I came back home. Well then, I wasn't so keen to go back on the Fish Quay after having been in a factory and found that working from 7.30am to 5.30pm, that was your day over. So then I decided, right - they were just starting to build the estate up at West Chirton - I thought 'I don't think I want to go back on the Quay again because it was a hard life' - it was really hard, you know. And I thought - I'll try the factories. And I got a job in the British Die Casting. Of course, I was there for about seven years which was similar work to the metal side of Angus's again.

"There was a pay off. They took you - last in, first out, but I was lucky because the British Thomson-Houston was further down the road. I was lucky in as much as I came from the Die Cast and I got the whisper that they were starting one or two girls for the power presses. So, on my way from work, went in and was lucky and I met the Personnel Manager as he was coming out to go home. However, I had an interview. On the Monday morning I got started, and I was with the B.T.H. power press work".

I asked if this was skilled work. Vera: "You see, women are never skilled, not in the sense of men. There were no apprentices in that light engineering. It's only this last few years, since the equality, that a woman has been allowed to go in for an apprenticeship. But in those days, as long as you were capable and you did a good job you kept going. Plus the fact that it was piecework, which was a great incentive. From the Die Cast the money was pretty good there. But when I got into the B.T.H., having done the same work during the war on big power presses, that was the job I got there. So I more or less went in as skilled - in as much as a woman could be skilled - I was an experienced operator.

"B.T.H. made parts of aircraft but Coventry was our head and we made lots of components that were sent to Coventry to be assembled. So it was more or less the component side that we did and then it went on to the parent factory. Well, I was there about 14 years, made lovely money: a grand job. Then again, a few of the girls I had worked on the Fish Quay with and travelled with, they were there as well. We more or less brought a little bit of the singing lark into it you know, and it worked out very well".

Inside the British Die Casting factory, 1959 and, right, the exterior of the premises in 1948.

"Well, unfortunately the work, the aircraft side of it, was getting very, very bad and the A.E.I. [Amalgamated Electrical Industries] took it over. We were put into one small part of the whole factory to do small components, the sort of finishing off. And then it came the crunch, that everything was going back to Coventry. So we were the first women - or part of a factory, in the north east - you know when the redundancy came on the thing. We were the very first factory to be made redundant with payment.

"Now I was lucky in as much there again. We were given a good notice... when we went down to the dole we got the chance - Ronson was opening a big factory at Cramlington, but till that was ready they wanted a small division here [North Shields] for to make hair dryers... As it happened we finished work on the Monday, started work on the Tuesday morning. So I was straight - I mean it doesn't happen now - but then things worked out very well for me. We went in, we went training, making these hair dryers. Well, it turned out, I fell in, they wanted a chargehand. During the first month they must have been watching out and

they decided I was the one, so I got the chargehand's job. There was a chap above me and between the two of us we ran this hairdryer division at West Chirton. They had 54 girls working there, which was good. But you can get one or two girls in that 54 who can make life very, very unpleasant for you. But I got over that because I rather liked the job, plus the fact - well, then, I was 48 - 47/48-year-old, and I thought for me to be made Supervisor - I felt a little bit chuffed about it! We knew when we started, mind, that this job was only going to be for two years because they were building this big factory at Cramlington whereby they wanted their electrical toothbrushes, and shavers, hairdryers, everything, under one roof."

Vera's experiences of factory work reflect the industrial history of the north east. The heavy industry associated with the work of 'the Die Cast' declined, and so she was paid off. Industries with branch factories established in development areas like the north east tended to retract to their base in times of difficulty. The British Thomson-Houston accordingly transferred its work back to the parent factory in Coventry. Government policy and the

The Ronson factory in Cramlington in 1970. When it opened it provided new kinds of work for women as the demand for consumer goods increased.

rising demand for consumer goods in the 50s and 60s promoted light industry in the north east. This was partly to provide jobs for women in the area after the war. Hence Ronson's building their factory in Cramlington and Vera's recruitment into a hair dryer division. Vera also benefited from the government legislation designed to protect workers (Redundancy Payments Acts 1965) and, later, from efforts to reduce unemployment (the Job Release scheme).

Home Pressures

Industrial and economic change and government initiatives shaped Vera's experience of work in important ways, but personal and family influences shaped it even more powerfully "Well, as the time was coming for the factory to be finished, they asked me then, 'Would I care to go through to Cramlington, train some of the girls there?' Well, I did that daily, but unfortunately for me I was a terrible traveller, hopeless. From being a kiddie I was always bad... However, I was offered the Supervisor's job in this department. Really I was reluctant to turn it down because I liked it. Everything about it. They even went to the point - I said 'travelling, no way - no way'. They were very good - you see at the time the shipyard was getting a little bit dodgy and there was a chance that me husband would be made redundant and things were really at that bad pitch. But I said I couldn't go to work on a morning knowing I had to face that journey back home at night. So they said, 'We can even get you a house on the Cramlington estate'. I says, 'Ah, it's one thing me moving house for me husband's benefit. But, I says, 'No way, if he can keep his job in that shipyard, he's going to keep it, and no way would he travel'. So of course I had to turn it down."

The fact that her husband's attitudes caused her to have to turn it down illustrates how the traditions of north eastern life were more powerful than the ideas of industrial planners and managers. Clearly she was upset at having to give up this job and had no heart for applying for another. But a few weeks of being unemployed were enough to show her that she did not like to be without a job.

Clearly, her life at work was very important to Vera. She had no children, which was a sadness to her. She said, "I love children, and I've always tried to help people who have got children, same with elderly people. I mean, the way things happened with me mother - there was me own father, me mother, and me stepfather, and I had the three to nurse. So I said, 'Ee, the good Lord puts you on earth for some purpose and obviously that has been mine'".

In saying this, Vera reflected the strong sense of responsibility for caring for elderly relatives which was part of the north east's tradition. Vera here interprets the purpose of her life in terms of being there to care for her older relations and not in terms of her working life. But when it came to a choice she found that looking after her mother was, on its own, not satisfactory. She needed the stimulus of work, probably more than the money that it brought.

Because she had no children of her own, the question of whether to have a job did not arise for her in the way that it arose for many women. Perhaps, surprisingly, her husband does not seem to have felt that he should keep her, or that for her to have a job would be a slight on his capacity as a wage earner. This question probably did not arise since she had been working consistently for so long before they married and because they, no doubt, expected that when they had children, this would settle the question. The only time when the question of whether she should have a job arose was when Vera had to turn down the job

as supervisor. "But I was at the stage then when I thought, 'Ee, well, I could do with a break'. Course my mother was getting older, she needed a little bit more attention, so I thought, 'No, we've got to stay in this area'. So again, they closed the plant down and I thought, 'Well, I'm going to have a couple of months on the dole'... I was on the dole, oh, I would say a month. I thought. 'A month, it's enough for me', having been used to being working all the time. So a friend of mine worked at Angus's and she said, 'Why don't you come and have a go up there?' Well, again, I think because of past experience, I got the job at Angus's. So I came off the dole after only a few weeks more or less, and here I get started at Angus's. I was there till I retired!

"I used to finish me day's work, and then it used to start! I'd go straight to me mother's, do what had to be done there, come home, collect shopping, see to the evening meal, prepare lunches to take to work next day. So me time was pretty well taken up. Weekends: we used to get out quite a lot on a weekend because I would rather during the week come in and do me housework at nights; do what me mother had to have done at nights, if I possibly could, leaving the weekend free to do, you know, the social side of it.

"In Angus's, mind, I loved it! I liked it. I got to the stage, Caroline, where, as time was getting on, I had to go part-time because me mother was in very bad health. Now, I worked that so that there's a friend of mine - she had two young children and she couldn't get out to work. So I saw Personnel and the foreman, and between us it was decided that I should go part-time. So what I did, I got me friend to come in and see to me mother on a morning, while I went to work. Well, me wages I used to come home with, I used to split that down the middle, and it meant I still had my bit job, and it was giving a little bit job for Betty, who couldn't. So that worked very, very well till eventually me mam died. And the foreman put me back on full-time again, and I was there until I came out on Job Release. I came out at 59.

"And that was it. I just sort've been retired and enjoying it since then, as much as the healthwise part of it lets me, you know. But I am... I've sort of got myself involved in one or two little things... a couple of old dears used to live down the street in the flats - a couple of old dears down there. I was popping in and seeing to them and things like that. And one of them went to the Willows and I made it a point of going there and seeing her you

"I mean there's nothing that can compare with the Fish Quay. The environment that you worked in. You stood in yards where, because of the nature of your work, the heating was limited, so it was a very, very cold place to work in."

know: But taking it by and large... and you see all the years when I did work I used to pay the big stamp so consequently when I came out on this Job Release I went from me Job Release straight on to me retirement pension."

When Vera's mother died it was a "terrible thing" in her life. She had had to nurse her for four years, during which time she became senile and like a baby to deal with, in addition to being stone deaf. So when she died, "it was like a child going out of the house". At the last, she went into hospital for what did not seem a serious chest condition, and died within four days. Vera found this very difficult to accept and at first felt great anger with the hospital for having let this happen.

"Once the funeral and that was over, I couldn't get straight back on full time and I was coming home on a lunch time and, oh, the thoughts that used to go through my mind. I couldn't get myself organised in me mind somehow as to why she had died and, I did, I went through a pretty rough time".

At the end of 10 months, Vera herself had a serious heart attack and very nearly died. A few weeks later her stepsister had a heart attack and did die. When Vera was recovering, her doctor helped her to come to terms with her mother's death by giving her a "rollocking" and saying, 'After all, Vera, your Mam didn't die a bad death, and you managed to cope while you had your mother. If this had happened when she was alive where would

you have been then?' "He helped me through, the way through that because, ee, it was bad, Caroline, those months. I never thought anything of it while I had me mother and I was doing for her. I had to do it. I was her daughter and I just did it. But it wasn't till I lost her... and that few months I was left there and I felt high and dry".

After the heart attack and getting over it... "I had an entirely different outlook on things and even when people say to me, 'Have you not got any family'? 'Ah, no, the Lord didn't choose to give me any children'. But at least he's given me good friends and I do firmly believe that, because I'm very fortunate. I've got, I would say three - don't sit over me, very seldom I see them, but they're genuine friends. It's just a case of picking the phone up and they're there and they help when they can".

In her retirement, Vera enjoyed looking after her neighbour's little girl and going out on expeditions with her in the school holidays. This gave Vera some of the enjoyment of being a grandmother. It also enabled her neighbour to go out to work - the cycle of Tyneside women's experience of work began again.

Reflections on Vera's Story

If in one sense Vera speaks for Tyneside, in another she speaks specifically for North Shields. The fact that she came from this town associated with the fishing industry, meant that working on the Fish Quay was one of the options open to her, as working at the Pelaw Co-op factories, at Maling's potteries or Reyrolles were for the women who came from other districts of Tyneside. Although the underlying cultural and industrial assumptions were common to the whole of Tyneside, the fact that the women in the study, of which Vera's story forms a part, came from particular districts meant that particular work opportunities were natural to them.

The intention of this book is to be both faithful to the personal experience of the women upon whose accounts it was based and, at the same time, to explore the ways in which this personal experience was shaped by the state of the economy, government policy and other wider influences.

Photo opposite: Children learning sewing skills at Whickham View School, c1943.

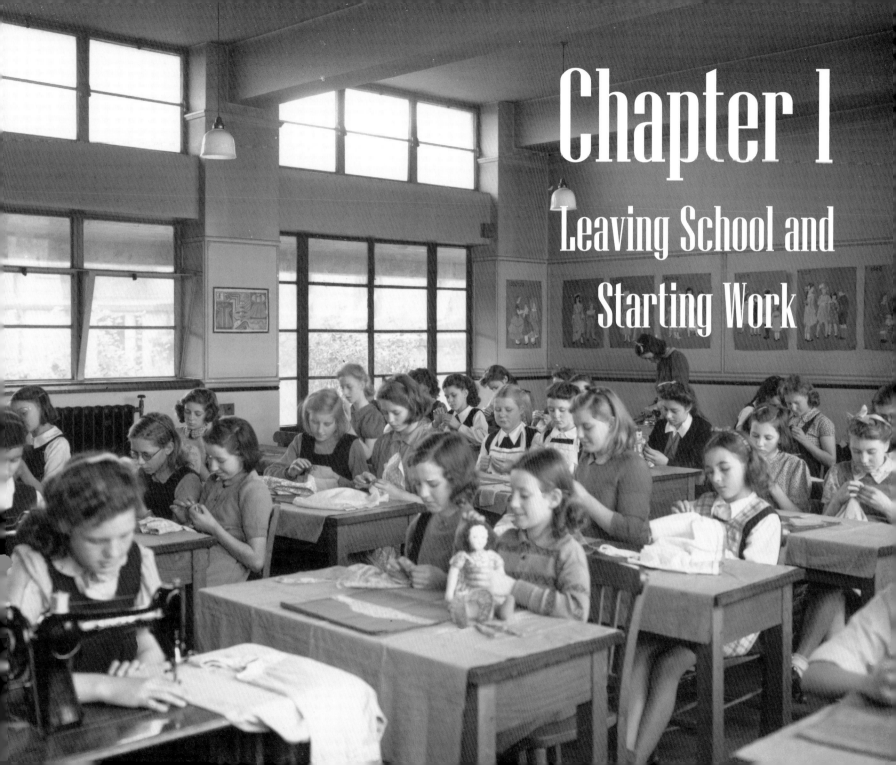

Chapter 1
Leaving School and Starting Work

I started my conversations with the women by asking about how they entered the world of work when they left school: what jobs they had gone into and what careers advice they had had. They told me about their experience of moving from school to work and thus into the adult world; how they got their bearings in the world of work and began to make some choices of their own even though in a limited range of opportunity.

Although they were leaving school in the apparently very different worlds of Tyneside in the 1930s, the post-war period and the recession of the 1980s, their experience included a strong common core. Nearly all would have said of their workplace what Margaret said of Maling's pottery in 1939, "It was just a place you went to".

They left school between 1934 and 1981 and all at the minimum school leaving age. It was only the youngest who found any difficulty in finding work. Even in the 1930s there were jobs for girls although it might mean going into service or swallowing your pride and taking a job in a factory like Tyne Brand or the Rope Works - a notoriously tough place for women workers, known as "Haggies' angels".

Those who left school in the 1950s and 60s found a labour market needing them in retailing and factories, especially in clothing and in the light engineering works on the new industrial estates.

Careers Advice

What kind of advice from the Careers Service, or before it from the Youth or Juvenile Employment Service, would have been available to the young women? Until the 1973 Employment and Training Act, local education authorities (L.E.A.s) had a choice about whether to be involved in the Service, which was entirely the responsibility of the Ministry of Labour. On Tyneside, Newcastle Education Authority had a strong commitment to being involved and had been so since 1911. The LEAs had a more person-centred approach to the task and had easier access to schools. The Ministry of Labour had to seek permission from the Director of Education for its officers to interview young people in schools.

Trades for Tyneside Girls, published in 1950 by Newcastle Education Committee.

Between 1947 and 1950 Newcastle Education Committee produced a series of booklets: *Trades for Tyneside Boys* on: *Engineering, Shipbuilding, Furnishing, Coachbuilding.* The foreword to the first volume includes the following good advice: "It is most unwise to drift into acceptance of the first vacancy offered without considering what it demands from the boy in the way of qualifications and what it offers in the way of prospects. Choice, not chance, should direct him into employment."

Only one, *Trades for Tyneside Girls,* was produced (in 1950) - on Laundering, Dyeing & Cleaning. In view of the assumptions about girls and employment at the time, it is not surprising that nothing was said about choosing a job with good prospects. Instead, what might seem a rather dredged-up enthusiasm for the trade in question was offered: "For many girls there is a special attraction in working with articles of clothing. Many factory workers find their own part in the whole productive system is so small that the job itself has little intrinsic interest. Laundry workers, however, have the satisfaction of working with articles of personal wear or household use and can take a genuine pride in achieving a high standard of cleanliness and finish"!

The employment prospects for young people before and after the Second World War were very different. Kenneth Roberts, in his book about the Youth Employment Service, *From School to Work*, writes in the section on the thirties, "School leavers who were fortunate enough to have relatives or friends in influential positions in industry were often able to fit themselves up in the more desirable types of jobs that were available, but the many young people who did not possess such useful contacts would be constantly presenting themselves at the juvenile employment bureau. In such circumstances, giving detailed vocational advice and guidance to young people who were still at school was hardly a practical proposition... Since it was known that school leavers would have difficulty in finding any work at all, there could be little point in encouraging them to make their minds up carefully about exactly what type of employment they would like to obtain."

Writing in 1971, Roberts would not have known that what he was writing about the thirties would be applicable in the north east in the eighties. Contrasting the situation just described with the situation after the war, he writes, "Employers have been obliged to offer decent prospects and conditions of work in order to attract young people. Blind-alley and casual employment have largely disappeared from the adolescent scene". All that he says no doubt applied more to boys than girls.

Whenever the women in this study left school, the careers advice they received seems to have been very similar. Margaret who left school in 1940 reported: "We did have people come to ask what we would like to be when we were leaving. Each one was interviewed and then they'd ask, 'Would you like to be typing or hairdressing or such as a domestic?' Although they asked me if I'd be a domestic and I definitely said 'No. Emphatically, No!' But I've ended up that way". (After being made redundant from Angus's she had taken a job as a hospital cleaner).

Pat left school in 1981 and said, "Oh aye, we got careers advice. But what I wanted they didn't have lessons in it. So I never bothered taking any exams and I started in my factory on the YOP two days after leaving school. I got let out on the Thursday afternoon instead of the Friday. I went to the Careers Office straight away and I started on the Monday. It was just a YOP (Youth Opportunity Programme) I got put on. I wanted painting and decorating but they didn't have it."

Pat started in a clothing factory and became a machinist. Clothing factories were a constant employer of women in the north east. June left school in 1944: "Careers people had just started to come to the schools then. And the teacher suggested that I was good at sewing in class and she suggested that that's the kind of work I should do. So I got a green card from the careers woman who came to the school and I started at Pelaw, that's where I served me time".

Nancy left school in 1958. Her mother came with her to the Careers Office: "But the man says there's nothing really I could go in for like specialising in nursing, because I didn't have any qualifications". However, "there were millions of jobs, just for the picking". Nancy had a choice between "a job in the sweet factory with the rest of the girls out of me class"; a job at C&A [retail clothing store]; a job with a printer and bookbinder which a friend wanted her to go to and a job at the grocery store where she had a Friday night and Saturday job. The manager there "was really upset about it because I left." But her mother had a decisive influence: "Me Mam said, 'No, you're not. You're just going to the sweet factory for the sweets. I don't mind you going to work in C&A's but bookbinding... I would rather you take up a career that you could always fall back on and earn yourself some money and do something to help yourself.' So she made us go to Clay's [a clothing factory] and I got a job there."

When I asked Jeanette if she had any careers advice before she left school in 1950, she laughed and said, "Oh no! First I went to Catholic School, which taught in those days a lot of religion, Caroline, you see. And you weren't really encouraged in any way because the most thing they wanted you to be encouraged to be was a good Catholic." Living in Felling, as she did, the Co-op factories at Pelaw were an obvious place to go to work, "Everybody where I lived went to work at Pelaw, where the Co-op factories stretched right along". People worked "either in tailoring, the shirt making - I think there was a food part. There was blankets and sheets and there were all different things - oh, and there was handbags and suitcases. They made everything there. Well, me mother was absolutely horrified at the thought of us going into a factory or anything, you see. So I worked - I fancied myself you see - in a nice... a shop, not a grocery shop, something nice. So I went to Binns [a department store in central Newcastle]. It was quite easy to get in at the time."

Binns in central Newcastle was seen as a nice shop to work in and, below, Cail and Sons on the Quayside, where Sally found employment in the 1960s.

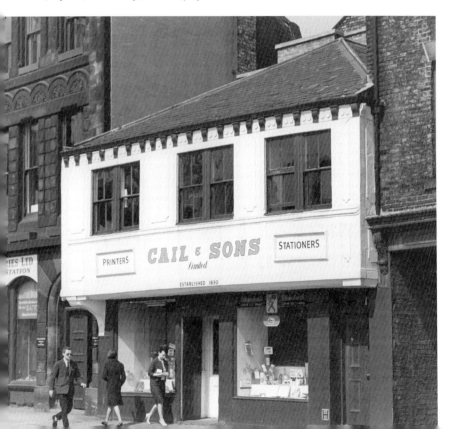

The Influences Affecting Choice

Their mothers were often a decisive influence on where they went to their first job. Alice left school in 1945 just after the war ended. Her mother wanted her to work in an office so her first job was in a local office of what became the DHSS {Department of Health & Social Security). "But I got me own way at the finish. Most of my friends were in sewing, things like that, and, I don't know, I'd rather fancied doing something like that. I was always good at making things." Like Jeanette, she got a job at Binns in the dressmaking workrooms.

Brenda, leaving school in 1957, didn't get her way with her mother. "I fancied being a - you'll laugh when I tell you this like - I fancied being a prison wardress when I left school and I wrote away for the information. But it was Mam who wouldn't let us go. She said, 'Some queer characters get in there and you're not going to be punched around and badly used'. So, it all went into the fire". Instead, a relative spoke for her and she got a job in a Co-op greengrocery. She could not remember getting help from the Careers Service, "No, I mean now it's fantastic. I think, the way, you know, kiddies can go and get help and taken and shown around places and try things, and they get loads of help with different types of jobs. I mean then, nobody ever bothered, probably because at that time there was stacks of work."

If mothers were the most important influence, family, neighbourhood and school tradition were also important. Rachel, leaving school in 1968, went to work in Angus's straight away and stayed there. "We went there on Careers Week when I was at school. Me sister worked there and so I wrote in before I left school. I got an interview, and I got the job. I was left school about a fortnight before I started working". She couldn't remember having other jobs suggested and it seems it was a matter of course to go to the factory which was just across the road from the school. The factory's Training Officer was a school governor for many years and, when Rachel started, four other girls from the school started at the same time. She did not mention if any boys started apprenticeships or unskilled jobs at the same time, but it seems quite likely that they did.

Julie followed family tradition when she left school in 1964 and became a machinist. "Actually, I wanted to be a hairdresser.

"We went there on Careers Week when I was at school. Me sister worked there and so I wrote in before I left school. I got an interview and I got the job. I was left school about a fortnight before I started working."

Rachel describing how much of a factor family was in determining young women's employment decisions.

The staffroom at the Louise Argyle factory in Hebburn.

But when I found out how much the wages were going to be, I changed me mind." In hairdressing she would have been paid £1. 10s per week as against £3.6s.8d in the clothing factory. How did she choose clothing? "Well, I think I just sort of done what me sisters done, you know. I thought, 'Well, if it's good enough for them, like, it's good enough for me, sort of thing.'"

Sally also followed her sisters, starting work in 1966. Her initiation into work started before this when she was fourteen and was taken by her sister to join NATSOPA (National Society of Operative Printers & Assistants). Her sisters were in the print: "so I was forced to join the Union when I was fourteen. I never wanted to be a printer, hated it. All me sisters were. I went straight into the printing trade. I left school on the Friday night. On the

Monday morning I was away with me bait in me hands, up the street, me Mam crying and waving and what have you! So I started a kind of apprenticeship at Cail & Sons, the printers on the Quayside."

Unlike the other women, Yvonne had a clear determination when she left school in 1975 to work with horses. "I knew I wanted to do that from when I was young. I always liked horses. I've ridden since I was five. I just knew that I didn't want to do anything else".

She had lived in the country near Winchester where there were horses. But her father having died, by the time she was ending her schooldays, she lived in north Northumberland. Her first job was training to be a girl groom in hunting stables in the

Borders. She heard about the job through a friend who gave her a lift to the interview by "the head man of the stables". Yvonne "had been with horses a lot of years" and had worked part-time in a riding school, so she was given the job. She started immediately and after she had been there a week, her mother came to see if she wanted to stay. "We had a little cottage but it wasn't very good. There was no carpets on the floors and when me mother saw it she didn't want me to stay. But I wanted to, because I wanted to work with horses, you see. There were six girls - three in each bedroom."

The Limitations of Choice

Many of these accounts show the tug the young women felt between their family's desire for security and respectability and what they might personally have wanted. But on the whole it seems there was little friction, perhaps because the options cannot have seemed very great. Typically, they left school at the end of one week and started work the next.

Phyllis, the oldest of the women, left school and started work on her fourteenth birthday in 1934. The four shillings a week she earned as a maid-of-all-work was vital to the family finances as her father was out of work. She ran home twice when it got too much for her, but her mother took her back, saying she couldn't leave without another job to go to. I commented on this, that at least she was needed as a worker unlike her young relation who was currently going through a long period of unemployment. When I saw her the next week, she said,"Last week when you said... I thought about it afterwards ... that even... I was needed even for that small thing. It wasn't that I was needed. It was the money that was needed."

Since she started work in the thirties this was more the case with Phyllis than for those who started work in the more affluent post-war period. However, one gets the impression from these accounts that the people I was talking with were seen by schools, the Careers Service and families as inevitably part of the unskilled workforce and the choice mostly boiled down to factory or shop. This was not an adequate description of the women that I knew and of their capacities and potentialities as human beings.

In effect the educational and social system of the country failed to offer them chances for self-development, whether in times of low or high unemployment. Their opportunities for development as human beings came from their experience of being workers; through relationships of all kinds, including experience as mothers; through trade union practice and education; through going on holiday; and through what they have gained from such things as television, reading and evening classes.

How these developments occurred will emerge in what follows. It is important to remember how much this grew from their being able to enter jobs as young people leaving school. It was through this experience that they began to mature into adults. Young people faced with long periods of unemployment and therefore with little or no money, find many of the avenues to maturity and a place in society blocked.

"Careers people had just started to come to the schools then. And the teacher suggested that I was good at sewing in class and she suggested that that's the kind of work I should do."

Alice on how she was directed towards the clothing industry.

Photo opposite: Women working at the John Sinclair tobacco factory in Bath Lane, Newcastle, 1949.

Chapter 2
Becoming Workers

1603

Reactions to the First Job

Some of the women remembered the business of starting work as a transfer to a tougher life than that of school. Rachel, starting at Angus's in 1969, felt: "Ee, I'll never stick this because getting up dead soon in the mornings, you know. First few days I felt like crying 'cos I was that tired. But it just grew on you. I'm just used to it".

What were her first impressions of the place? "Well, I don't know really. I just stuck it and that was it. I never thought, like, 'Crumbs, I think I'm going to be a dole wallah here', 'cos they told you 'Well, it's hard work'. But when you first went there you didn't go on piecework till you were eighteen. I was a service operator and you were pushing the barrows up till you were eighteen when you could go on piecework. And I just stuck it."

Perhaps she was helped to stick it by her sister, who had worked in the factory for some time already, and by the fact that she started with friends from school. Situations where you did not know anyone were described by several of the women as being hard to bear.

Brenda also had a physically demanding first job: "I went to work [in 1957] in the Co-op for just over twelve month, in the greengrocery. It was supposed to be a sales assistant but I think I was that tall and hefty I got all the heavy humping work of sacks of potatoes and crates of bananas, and I was more just a filler-cum-packer of shelves than a sales assistant, you know. I can't ever remember being on the counter at all."

On the whole, those who went into shop work enjoyed it. Audrey, starting work in 1952, said,"From I left school I went into a shoe shop, the Co-op. That was a good job in them days, the Co-op. You got a job at the Co-op, you got a better wage, you see. So I was in the Co-op shoe shop and I worked there till I was about eighteen and that was when I got engaged, and of course I decided I'd work in a factory to get some more money. So then I went into Wills [in 1955] and instead of getting £3 a week I got £5."

Jeanette, speaking of her three years at Binns [1950-53] said, "I loved it. I was in the Children's Fashions. It was lovely." She got day release once a week, "for speech, believe it or not! For speech, arithmetic and English. We went to the College of Commerce. I liked it. It was good. I was in the Children's and at Christmas we got to work at a counter that sold toys."

Monica, leaving school in 1959, went to work in a department store in Byker. She enjoyed it because it was "a proper family business" and "quite homely." "It was a real busy shop then. They were always having sales." She was helped by the fact that she went there with three others from her class.

After two years she moved to a very traditional shoe shop in Wallsend. The owner was the manager and "on a Monday morning there was a timetable and each week you were on a rota and you had to dust every shoe box in the shop. Open them up. Check that the pair inside was one size and then put clean paper in and then move all of the spaces down where they had been sold."

The assistants were not allowed to talk or eat and they had to wash the chairs and the floor on their hands and knees. "He was very clean about his shop. He catered for all the family from the babies up to the grandparents 'cos a lot of the shops don't do that now. It's all fashion. He didn't have much trend in there!" In spite of this regime Monica enjoyed working there. "I liked the shoe shop because you could get a pair of shoes every week - pay weekly." She left to have her first child.

Learning and Surviving in the World of Work

Acquiring the disciplines and know-how of particular jobs and workplaces is obviously important in entering the world of work. This came out most strongly in the accounts of those who went into factory or production work. When Julie started at the clothing factory in 1964 she said, "I hated it. I couldn't stand it. For the first, I would say, five or six weeks, I cried every night when I went home and I used to say to me mam, 'I'm not going back. I can't stand it'. And she would say to us, 'If you find another job you can leave that one'.

When Julie started, several other girls started at the same time, but she didn't know any of them. "You were at everybody's beck and call. You had to run around after everybody, which I wasn't used to doing. I mean even at home I didn't sort of pull me weight which I should've done. Course, you blame your mother for that, don't you? You're not made to do it! But I think that's what I didn't like about it, you know, people saying 'Do this, do that, do the other; get us this, get us that'. I just didn't like that part of the job. At first I just didn't think I fitted in, you know, but after a few weeks I got used to it."

As we have heard, Vera also had to work her way in when she went to work on the Fish Quay in 1935. First she had to learn skill and speed. Then she was able to move from one employer to another.

Sally did not enjoy her apprenticeship in printing starting in 1966. She gave a graphic account of how she felt about it. On the way to work she "used to have to pass the doss house and all the tramps, you know, at seven o'clock in the morning. It was terrifying! I stuck it out for nearly two years and then broke.

"Your first couple of years you're just a general dogsbody, you know. But you had to learn how to set the machines up, put the rollers in place, the type in place; papers, you know, the reams of papers, what have you, washing them down, going for typesets. Getting the compositor to check over after you had printed them. But, as I say, you're just a general dogsbody, standing over people, watching them, which I didn't like. Plus it's very boring. Because you used to have a machine the size of a living room and you had like a little ledge to walk round. And you used to have to get inside of it and things like that. But you used to have to watch it and you used to be sitting. It was little dark rooms and you were just bored to tears and I would look up sometimes and the paper was sky high to the ceiling where I'd never been watching it, and it just ravelled and ravelled. And I just didn't like it."

This experience seemed to have, for Sally, a nightmarish quality. But she did complete her three-year apprenticeship by moving to another company, where she also learned bookbinding. "I liked the bookbinding side of it - that was good. You not only numbered pages, you collated the pages. The only thing you didn't do was your own guillotine work. You used to hand-stitch them in their leaves, collate them, bind them, gold bond, you know. But it wasn't very often we were let loose on the gold bond because it was very expensive!"

The experience of starting work as being a step into the adult world was most clearly expressed by Alice. Although she hadn't really wanted to work in an office, she enjoyed her job as a clerical assistant in 'the Ministry', starting in 1944. "I was going to pass exams to be a C.O. (Clerical Officer) but I didn't stay long enough

for that. It was just more or less helping out - change of address, things like that. I enjoyed it. Of course I was young and, you know, the novelty of working and so forth." When she moved to the dressmaking section of a department store: "I used to go down with the head designer and, Oh, I used to feel ever so important because I had a little band on me wrist with pin cushions on and the tape measure and I was ever so important! We used to fit them and take all the measurements down, and that was my job - writing down all the measurements." She left after eighteen months because the only other young girl left. That didn't suit me then. I wanted to be with younger ones."

For both Vera and Margaret it was not a matter of the adult world of work being a step away from the family, for both went to join members of their families at work. Vera joined her mother on the Fish Quay in 1935 and Margaret went to Maling's pottery in 1939. Except for one of Margaret's younger sisters, "the whole family worked there" - parents, sisters and three aunts. "It was just a place you went to. The family looked after them. You didn't have any trainee or training instructor in them days. It was either your cousin or your aunt or your uncle who taught you." So the teaching about the disciplines of work and skills and conventions of the workplace were in the hands of other members of your family and no doubt the management relied on this system.

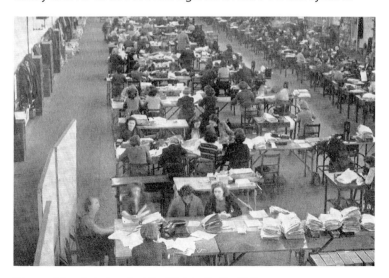

Women doing clerical work at the 'Ministry' in the 1940s.

In the 1980s, when I was an industrial chaplain at Angus's, the system was still partly in operation. In the face of high unemployment, the company might be inclined to take on the sons and daughters of existing workers. I did hear other workers being critical of the parents because the children had developed bad habits of shoddy workmanship or bad timekeeping.

The importance of families in job-finding and training was also found to be important in Griffin's study of young women in Birmingham in 1979: "The families of young working class women played an important role in their job-finding through informal contacts in local workplaces. Employers were wary of taking on school leavers, even as relatively cheap labour, but they were more likely to do so if there was some adult (preferably a relative) who would vouch for and discipline the young person if necessary."

For those who went into the clothing trade, the big issue in relation to becoming a worker was "getting on a machine". This meant persuading the boss. June, starting in 1944, was put on tacking to begin with. "You had to be sixteen before they would let you go on the machines, but I used to sneak on the zig-zag machine. When the foreman wasn't there one of me friends used to let us have a try. And they were a bit stuck for a canvas hand - it was making the canvases that go inside the jackets - and I asked Mr Wood. I says, 'Do you think, Mr Wood, I could go on the machines? I've been here nearly two...' (I wasn't sixteen, like, about fifteen and a half)... And he said, 'You cannot use the machine'. I says, 'I've been on a few times. I haven't told you, like, but I can do a canvas'. He says, 'Oh, can you now?' He says, 'Let's see you, like.' So I run one up and let him have a look at it and he says, 'Oh, aye, that's not bad'. Well they were stuck for a canvas hand 'cos she was off sick. So he says, 'Go on then, I'll let you have a go for a while - see how you do'. And I was on the machines ever since!"

Pat, on her YOP scheme, went (in 1981) to the factory where Pam was already working. Until she was put on a machine, Pat did not enjoy it much and used to take days off. "Like I started off on clipping. I was only on there for half a day and then I went on putting the pattern, drawing the pattern on to a pocket. I used to get bored with that after a bit. Once I've done something I lose interest in it straight away, me. So then this lass that was next to us, she used to iron the pockets. Then she started making the belt loops and cutting them. I got that job. And then, when I was bored with that, I started staying off again. And then I was packing this one day and they says I had been working hard so they tried us on a machine. And after that it was all right. I just kept going.... She [Pam] had been there longer than me but I got put on a machine first. They didn't give her a chance".

Caroline: "So why was that?"

Pam: "Because I was on clipping. There was a canny few on clipping, like, but... dunno... they just kept us on clipping. Then I started nagging him that I wanted to go on a machine, and so a couple of others started nagging him for us, and I got put on one."

When June started in clothing in 1944 she was paid £1.4s.9d a week. She gave her mother £1 and had to pay her fares out of the 4s 9d. "I never knew me father to work till the war started." He had worked as a baker in a bakery factory as a young man and then in a steel works, which closed. Her mother took in washing and washed for a butcher and his family. "Me brother and I used to carry them all back ironed in a basket. We used to get an apple! Those were the days!" Her mother used to get the family's clothes from a second-hand stall. "And they were good, because they were off - like what you would call - the rich people in Whitley Bay, 'deceased clothes', you know? And me mother used to wash and do them all up and that." When the war came a bomb factory was built on the site of her father's allotment but at least he got a job there! He would have been 63 in 1940.

Pat and Pam, living in the different social conditions of the 1980s, found managing on the £25 [YOP] allowance hard. Pat lived with her aunts who were cleaners in the shipyards. She gave them £10 a week. "I used to try and save up a bit from one week, and then save up a bit from the next week, until I had enough money for to buy a pair of jeans, like. It was the only way you could do it because it's just terrible on a YOP."

Pam said, "Me £10 board and £2.50 for me mam, and me tabs [cigarettes] you really couldn't afford even for to buy new clothes 'cos you only had about £10 left to yourself on a week... I had a part-time job on a Saturday, working in a shop and I used to get money from that. I think that's how I done it." When Pat got taken on as a regular employee, she got £34 flat at age 16 in 1982, £42 at 17 and £48 at 18.

Julie, who hated the first weeks in her clothing factory, found she enjoyed it after she got on a machine. After the first three months on the factory floor learning the ropes, she should have gone into a training school but her supervisor "decided she should learn us herself and I sort of got on a machine quick. She taught us everything really and after that I loved it. I was there ten year."

She enjoyed the challenge of piecework: "Once I was 16 (in 1964) you went on to piecework, and so every day was a challenge. You started the day with nothing. You had ... sort of... to make your own money then. 'Course £4 and £5 a day then was a lot of money. You were top wage earners if you were making £20/£25 a week. You were then the higher income bracket, and I could make it no bother. 'Course I had to work hard, mind." The hours were 8am - 4.45pm and there was a lot of opportunity for overtime. "You could work every Saturday if you wanted." Julie did so often. After ten years she just gave in her notice for no reason. Even looking back, she was not sure why. "I was married then, like, and I thought mebbe's a little rest from work. I couldn't! I was off a week and I got another job."

Nancy had quite an easy time settling into the clothing factory that she went to in 1958. "There was quite a few from our school started. I was put on the first day on the button machine and the girl showed us how to do the buttons, ee ... and I got carried away. I thought it was fantastic!"

After spells on the buttonhole machine for men's pyjamas and the trousers for men's pyjamas, "the manageress for the Marks & Spencer's team came down with the boss and she was looking for decent machinists for to be Marks & Spencer's girls. 'Cos if you're a Marks & Spencer's girl they thought they were above the pyjamas and the shirts. So they took me up to the elite and from there I was just just a Marks & Spencer's sewer." There she made girls' pyjamas, baby doll pyjamas, "mostly gym blouses. Everything had to be spick and span. 'Cos you're a Marks & Spencer's sewer and once you're accepted as one of them, that's it. You can go to a factory and tell them you're a Marks & Spencer's sewer. I'd like a bit of card to say I was, but I haven't got one."

About 800 people worked in the factory. "It was a huge factory. It was airy, and the music just used to be on a couple of hours a day, so we used to have to sit and talk all day to pass the time - and tell stories, and if anybody went to the pictures, everybody else got to know about it. I was there till I was nineteen and I got engaged and I had to pay for me own wedding" (because of the ill health of her parents) "and I didn't know what I was going to do about it because the money wasn't very good and the bonus was nothing really." In the end she took a job at the Plywood factory, which turned out to be an unpleasant contrast to the clothing factory.

Starting work had a powerful impact, as these descriptions show. For some, it was an enjoyable experience, but Rachel, who said she "just stuck it", summed up the feelings which many conveyed of being plummeted into a situation in which they felt powerless but to which there was little alternative.

If they had had a limited choice of what kinds of work to go into, they had little choice once they were inside about determining anything about the tasks they were given to do, the position they worked in or work patterns. Any idea of some kind of career development was really absent. Apart from those in clothing who hoped "to get on a machine" or those who waited to be old enough to get on piecework, there was no suggestion that the present had to be endured because it would lead to a brighter future. The feeling was nearer to that described by Simone Weil in her book *Waiting on God*: "When an apprentice gets hurt, or complains of being tired, the workmen and peasants have this fine expression: 'It is the trade which is entering his body'".

It was only by keeping a sharp eye open for opportunities that the women were able to exert some power over their situation in their workplace. Their other option was to move to another. June had to wheedle the foreman into allowing her on to a machine (this came out in the tone of voice she used in describing her encounter with him). Vera, on the Fish Quay, played the system by moving from one yard to another and Sally took advantage of the power of print workers, at the time, to move from one firm to another.

The First Moves

Some settled into the first workplace they went to but others came to a time when they decided to make a move. This was for a variety of reasons: Audrey and Nancy moved into factory work that they didn't enjoy to earn more money when they got engaged. Alice took the advantage of the closure of her office to move into the dressmaking work that she fancied and her mother had reservations about.

Brenda moved after a year in the greengrocery, not so much because of the work itself but because it was interfering with her social life. "A lot of friends that I knocked around with, they had factory jobs and they didn't work on a Saturday, and with we having these motor scooters at the time, which was all the go, they wanted to go away for weekends.

"I found that I was either the bugbear of them not going anywhere because I couldn't get a Saturday off, or they used to go, and I, if I wanted to go, had to go, like, to Hexham on me own and that, later on a Saturday night, which seemed to take the thrill and the fun and everything out of it 'cos they had been away in the morning and put all the tents up and, you know, I think you miss the best part of the fun and the carry-on by then. That was what made us write after the factory job."

Although she enjoyed her job at Binns, Jeanette moved after three years to a high-class grocer's shop, where a friend of hers worked. There she was given a lot of responsibility for dealing with money and the wages.

After her six months' training period at the hunting stables, Yvonne had to leave. She went back to work at the stables in Northumberland where she had worked before. "It seemed funny coming back to there. They seemed like little ponies!" She was only paid £10 a week and her board (this was 1976). The work was only seasonal so she would have had to move after the summer. In fact she met her future husband when he came for a holiday in a caravan on the site belonging to the stables. At the end of the summer it was arranged that she should go to live with his family in Wallsend. Thus she left the work with horses that she had always loved and took a job at Angus's after eight weeks on the dole. "I was quite pleased when I got a job there. It was totally different. Me mother said I wouldn't stick it!"

Vera, having got as far as she could in the work on the Fish Quay, took an opportunity to see wider horizons when she joined the "travelling shop". Her experience of travelling round the country was an unusual one for a girl from Tyneside. Thus she was in Gourock when war broke out and was conscripted into the torpedo factory.

For some of those who were working when the war started it proved to be the opening to a wider life. Phyllis had already managed to escape from domestic service to a job in a cafe in Whitley Bay, first as a still-room maid and then as a waitress. She volunteered as a dining-car attendant on the railways in the war. Thus she broke into working with men and was paid a man's wage. When dining-cars were taken off as food got scarcer, buffets, run by the men, were substituted. Phyllis was sent to be a station hand and booking clerk at Percy Main station. It entailed climbing the gantries to clean the signal lamps which her female colleague refused to do. It seems ironical that it was felt that women could do this job but not serve on the buffets! Eventually she volunteered for the army where she learned to drive - a useful skill, which got her a job when she was demobbed.

Margaret, working in the pottery, saw the wartime advertising films for the Land Army. "I just thought that joining the Land Army was seeing new worlds." However, it proved to be a struggle to be allowed to go since her employer had to sign the form to release her. "By heavens, they wouldn't let me out of that Maling's pottery!" Eventually she got her way and was sent to Bedfordshire, "I thought it was abroad then!" Across the water [i.e. the Tyne] you were abroad!"

These accounts of becoming workers demonstrate the strong orientation to disciplined hard work which has been part of the culture of the north east. Although this culture was determined by male employment, expectations of what being a worker entails had been assimilated by the women as well. It was only Pat, on a YOP scheme, who spoke about "staying off". This was, perhaps, the first suggestion, in the 1980s' world of high youth unemployment, of the breakdown of the assumptions about work-culture that were so clearly held by the older women.

Belonging to the world of work was traditionally a passport to adult society but belonging to adult society also determined the lives of the women. The assumption was that they would get married and have children so their lives as workers were of secondary importance.

Photo opposite: The Osram Lamp Works on the Team Valley in 1956.

Chapter 3
Shop & Factory

Suitable Jobs for Girls

Some of the women went to work in factories at the beginning of their working lives; others moved later on. Whenever they made the decision to work in a factory it was an important one.

For one thing, there was a social stigma attached to factory work or, more precisely, to women factory workers. This came out in the pull towards shop or office work the women felt when they were first choosing jobs. Their mothers, who were such a strong influence, were often reported as being against factories and in favour of shops or offices. Why was this? It was not the money, for factory work was better paid. It was not career prospects: the only person who mentioned career prospects was Nancy's mother who vetoed the sweet factory because: "You're just going for the sweets"; didn't mind C&A; was not keen on bookbinding but encouraged her to go into clothing because it was "a career that you could always fall back on and earn yourself some money and do something to help yourself."

The likely unspoken thoughts here were that she assumed Nancy would marry and have children and that in the event of difficulty or disaster she would probably be able to get a job in clothing. The shortage of labour in that industry was such that special provision was sometimes made for mothers with young children. Nancy's mother was right. Nancy was always being asked to come back to work once she was at home with her children and she did start work again when her children were young but fortunately this was not because of disaster or financial straits. It was more that people's expectations had changed: by the sixties more mothers were working to provide what would once have seemed luxuries but had become essentials. But this is to get ahead of ourselves into issues which faced the women at a later stage in their working lives.

The image of shop and office work was, if not glamorous, positive. They were seen as clean workplaces where you could wear nice clothes and be noticed. You might improve your social skills and your manners as you learned to serve customers and relate to other staff. Jeanette was sent to learn "speech", which underlines this aspect of shop work. You would meet a variety of people with the comings and goings of the life of office or shop and you might therefore meet a nice boy whom your mother would approve of your marrying. The hours would be regular. For some of those who took shop work, at least some of these things proved to be true.

For example, Audrey met her future husband who worked in an adjacent department at the Co-op. For others it did not: Jeanette had to work such long hours at the grocery that her fiance began to object. Brenda found that the shop hours conflicted with the social activities she shared with friends who worked in factories. For her, in any case, shop work had turned out to be heavy, dirty work.

The Worlds of Shop & Factory

Several of the accounts described the worlds of shops and factories and the ambivalence which those who moved from one to the other felt.

Audrey, having started with a job in the Co-op shoe shop, had a spell at Wills' cigarette factory in 1955 before going back into shops again. It was not the factory work itself that she disliked, but other aspects of the experience. "I didn't like Wills's. I hated it! I couldn't... I was very shy in them days, very quiet, and I found that going from a shop, where you were like a family, into a factory where there was maybe fifty girls working on an assembly belt... I just didn't connect with any of them. Whether they thought that I was trying to be a little bit posh because I was quiet - which I wasn't you know, I was just shy - and I didn't seem to be able to get on with any of them. Most of them were like me, they had had other jobs, but they had been factory girls. Then I felt they were a rough - you know, and I just couldn't get on with any of them. I used to speak to them all and be pleasant, but I couldn't make a friend and I felt really out, out of touch with them. Because in the shop we were all very good friends. We used to go out together and go to each other's houses. But in the factory I just couldn't make a friend. I think if I'd made one friend I could have stayed, but I stayed there for nine months and I didn't enjoy it at all.

"At Wills's then, you had to start off in what they called the Stemming Room. You had to make a quota each week, which I did, you know. I could do all the work. That was stripping the leaves and your hands used to swell and get very sore. It was hard

Wills' cigarette factory in 1965, where Audrey struggled to fit in with the other workers.

work but I could do it. But it was when you went for your lunch: I always felt as if I was pushing in with somebody that didn't want us. I didn't feel right. I wasn't comfortable working there at all".

In those days: "What happened was each floor went at a certain time in the morning - up two flights to the canteen. They all went together, like cattle! And sit down and eat your meal, your toast or whatever, for your breakfast as quick as you could, and then run back again. Very, very strict it was, very strict. If you went to the toilet and you were in the toilet more than a minute or so, the door was banged and you had to get out! There used to be an old dragon in the toilets. She used to shout,'Get out of there!' I wouldn't like to tell you what she used to shout! Well I thought it was terrible. I had never come upon anything like that in the shops. The manageress in the shop was lovely. She was like a mother. If you had a cold she used to give you a dose of Condey's Crystals, or whatever, to make you better, you know. When I went to the factory it was just entirely different and I just didn't fit in at all.

"At Will's I would say it was the only place I've really not got involved in anything... It might be hard to think it now, but I was then quite shy! I just didn't get involved, plus I was eighteen and I was engaged and of course when I went home I was wanting to go out with my boyfriend. So I wasn't really interested in going out with them girls. But I found Will's, of all the factories I've worked in, I would say it was more like a prison camp than anywhere else - very, very strict. If you didn't work on a Saturday morning, then you had to sometimes bring a doctor's note in to say why you didn't come in. It was really strict, which I think I could have taken, but I didn't mix with the girls at all. Unless I just started with a bunch of girls that were a bit rougher than the normal ones. But they weren't very nice girls and I wasn't used to language. You used to get a lot of swearing and... at the time I just wasn't a factory girl. I think factory girls have changed you know. I think now you get - factory girls when I was younger - usually a girl in a factory was 'common'!" Audrey laughed."This is the way people used to say 'Oh, she works in a factory, she's common'" [said in a superior tone]. "Granted they all weren't common but they were rougher than the girls I had been used to working with in the shop... I don't look on that as being a happy time at all."

Audrey tried to get her old job in the Co-op shoe shop back but there wasn't a vacancy. She put her name down in case one came up and took a job in Bon Marche on Wallsend High Street. "They started me in what they called the "Mantle Department" - ladies hats and coats, dresses, shoes. The wages were terrible, but I hated Wills so much, I went there. I think the wages were only £2.10s, which was only half the wage [at Wills]."

Audrey worked for a buyer: "She was a proper dragon. Oh, but in her way she was very kind to me but she was very, very tough. What she said was law. If she said,'Scrub that floor' you had to scrub it. Although you worked in a shop, you had to do exactly what she said. But I actually got on quite well with her and she put me in charge of the jumper department. I had all the nice jumpers to stack up and pretty blouses to sell and I quite enjoyed working there. But I had only been there about a year when I got a letter from the Co-op asking if I would go and work in their chemist's. So, of course, I jumped at the chance because I liked - the Co-op wage was better.

"So I went into the chemist, and I loved the chemist. I think of all the jobs I've ever had, the chemist was my job. I thoroughly enjoyed it. I enjoyed the nice smells and I enjoyed the nice - the travellers used to give you little gifts of soaps and lipsticks, and I just enjoyed it. But I was only there six months when my old boss in the shoe shop asked if I could go back to her because she needed someone to help out in the men's department. Well

Bon Marche on Wallsend High Street, where Audrey worked.

actually I didn't want to go because I liked the chemist better. But of course she had got on to the Secretary then, and he said I had to go. So then I went back to the original job again in the shoe shop, which I liked, but I preferred the chemist."

Caroline: "How could he tell you that you had got to go?"
Audrey: "Well, that was the way it was in them days. You had no choice. There was no union to speak of. I mean we paid w' union dues but we never ever... I couldn't even tell you who the union person was, you know. The Secretary was in charge and if he said, 'You go there', there's nobody you could ask to help you."

Audrey enjoyed the chemist because of her involvement with customers. "You met so many more people. The chemists was always busy from nine o'clock till... sometimes if you worked till seven it was busy all the time so you were kept busy, which I liked. And you had so many variations of things to serve, plus people who used to ask our advice and it was nice to talk to people who'd say, 'Now which cough bottle's the best, pet?' and things like this."

Audrey's account would have borne out just what the women and their mothers would have expected: the contrast between the prison-camp of the factory where people were shouted at and felt like cattle and the shop world, where your boss gave you cold cures and the atmosphere was that of a family; the contrast between the quieter, more friendly girls in the shops and the rougher, swearing girls in the factory. Even when I talked to Audrey, thirty years later, she still thought of the girls as rough. She recognised that she herself had changed but felt that "factory girls" in general had changed as well.

To the reader, the world of the shop may not seem to have been so clearly preferable to the world of the factory as Audrey felt it was. You could be ordered to scrub the floor; you could be posted from one job to another against your will, even by the Co-operative Society, which presumably saw itself as having the welfare of its staff as a priority. The canteen at Wills had an excellent reputation and the shop world provided no equivalent. But, for Audrey, the small-scale, intimate world of the shop and the contact with customers was better than the large, impersonal world of the factory.

Jeanette had a varied experience of shop work before she went into factory work. After three years in her first job in the department store, someone she knew got her a job where she worked: Brough's, a grocers in the centre of Newcastle. "When I started" [which would have been in 1953/54] "it was decided by someone that I would be better off in the office because there was only one woman there and she was about - I thought she was about ninety! - but she must have been about fifty-five - and a young girl. They put me in and she was very good. She taught us the wages and the income tax and all the invoices for the shop and she was really good. She left straight after, so I was there on me own with the young girl."

Caroline: "With all that responsibility?"
Jeanette: "Ee, yes. I used to have to take all the money to the bank, you know. All the money from all the tills of a night had to be right... I mean it wasn't self-service like nowadays. Everybody had to write a bill. I mean, even if you got, like, half a pound of butter, you wrote a little bill and the duplicates were kept and the duplicates had to reckon with all the money in the till (I used to go home reckoning up!) All by hand, I mean all by head, there was no calculators... It was just reckoning up. You wrote the bill out and you kept the duplicate. Now as they finished the little booklets they were kept. In one day, in another book, this thin book duplicated as well, I had to write every single price that had been done that day. On one page there was fifty and I had to reckon every page up... and all those pages were torn off and sent to Head Office with all the bills people had wrote. It was a terrible task! ... If I made mistakes I had to find it. I mean sometimes to do the day before's bills used to take me till lunchtime the next day. And if I made a mistake I used to have to take longer and of course, when Wednesday come, I had the wages. And then the bills for the things that came into the shop. I was in a perpetual state of harassment!"

This heavy responsibility was not recognised. "I only got the money what they got in the shop, that's all I got. And I mean the money we took that I handled every day and took to the bank, banked it, balanced the books with the wages and the tax and balanced the lot! You know, if it was, like, a shilling out, I mean, you'd think I'd committed a crime. And a pound! I mean, you dare be a pound out! I've seen me spend sleepless nights because I'd lost a pound... I mean it was hard. That was the hardest job I've ever had."

Caroline: "And I bet that has ingrained into you an ability you've never lost."

Jeanette: "Oh, that's how I reckon the wages up at work, you know, I do that pretty good - and the tax, when people can't understand their tax. The tax has never changed - how they work it out - you still have the book and the week, how much you can earn."

So the skill Jeanette learned in this demanding job in the shop, she put to use in her role as a shop steward, working out her own and others' earnings in a complicated piecework system.

"I got engaged, but I used to have to be always working late because I always had all these books to do. It used to be six o'clock and seven sometimes by the time I got the jobs I had to do in the day done, plus if anything had gone wrong the day before." Her fiance "went mad because first of all I never met him on time, he was always having to come and look for us. And he thought what I done, the hours I worked, was absolutely ridiculous for the money I got. I was twenty-one and I was getting £4 a week. So really I left because of that. I left and I didn't really have a job. But jobs - you could get them so easily!"

By 1957, Jeanette had got married and she got a job in a grocers at the end of the road where she lived. "It was only a small shop and it only had the manageress and this woman I knew - she lived near me - and a girl I went to school with, and me. But the manageress was bad-tempered and she hated my name, Jeanette, you see. She said, 'I can't call you Jeanette, I'll call you Jean' And I said, 'Well, please yourself, 'cos I won't answer you'. So of course she called me 'Jean' and I never answered her. And she used to say 'Girl' to us. So I didn't stay there. That was me worst job. I stayed just about four month".

The local food Co-op was advertising for assistants and Jeanette went there. "And I really liked it there. But it was funny there because you had to weigh everything in the Co-op in those days. There was great big sacks of flour and great big sacks of sugar and when you weren't serving you had to weigh all these things and you got really good at guessing a pound. Of course the Co-op was very busy. But the manager was... we shut at five, we shut prompt five because he used to have to get home and get his dinner to get to the pub!

Well, I enjoyed it there and I was married and the girls were all about my age, two of them I'd gone to school with, because Felling was then a very small place you know. It was just like a little village more or less then. It was before they built all the flats.

It was fields and I used to walk through the fields to work. I was never off - until this Wednesday. We used to finish at four o'clock on a Wednesday and I had gone home for me dinner. We got an hour. I used to walk home, which used to take twenty minutes and I had twenty minutes in the house. Me mother-in-law lived next door to us and, ee, I must have looked terrible because she come up and said, 'You're not going to work?' I said, 'Ee, I've got to, got to'. It was raining and she says, 'Ee, you must stay off' and she gave us whisky (I don't know what she thought the whisky would do!) and I was sick and I felt terrible and she said, 'You can't go to work. Get to bed'.

"I went to bed. The next day, I was so worried about this manager. I knew he was bad tempered and I thought 'I must go to work' and I felt desperate. And I went and said to him, 'I'm sorry I was off yesterday. I was poorly.' He said to me, 'I hope wherever you were you got soaked' I said, ' I was in bed'. He just walked away and I was upset and I thought, well, I had been there two years or three and I've never lost one day, never late. So I gave me notice in and I didn't have a job. But jobs, you see, were so easy to get."

One of Jeanette's sisters, Mary, had worked in more than one factory and was changing her job. She had an interview at Osram Lamps on the Team Valley Industrial Estate. Jeanette said, 'A factory! I wouldn't work in a factory.' But she agreed to go with Mary to her interview. "And of course the Personnel said to me 'Do you not want a job?' 'Oh', I said, 'I wouldn't work in a factory'. He said, 'Why?' ' Well, they're dirty and everything'. He said, 'Oh? Would you like to see one?' And I said, 'Well, yes, I wouldn't mind.' So he showed us round the factory. Well, I was really amazed because it was spotless. It was, really and it was lovely, lovely. So he said, ' Well, you've got a job if you want a start.' So I thought, 'Well, I'll give it a try.' Anyway, I started and it was the best job I'd ever had. I found that the worst for swearing and calling people behind their backs was Binns, the next was Brough's, listening to the girls who served in the shop. And the place I didn't hear any bad language at all was the factory, where they were mostly, I suppose, youngish married or unmarried, girls."

Jeanette's weekly wage in these jobs was: about £6.5s at the Co-op, which was about £1 more than she had got at the local grocers and £2 more than at Brough's. At Osram's she got £8 - a flat rate which you got for keeping up with the conveyor belt. This was in 1958/59. Looking back on this, Jeanette said, "Of course the wages in shops was absolutely disgusting. It was. And they could make you work. I mean, you didn't get overtime, Caroline, I mean, I could stay till seven o'clock and not get a penny and I had been there from nine - from half-past eight - I started at Brough's at half-past eight.... And sometimes if you reckoned how many hours you had worked in a week, I had worked sixty. I had been there sixty (at Brough's) and I only ever got £4."

Jeanette's experience of the world of shops was in some respects similar to Audrey's. They both enjoyed selling articles they liked themselves: Jeanette: the children's clothes and toys; Audrey: the nice jumpers and the cosmetics and cures at the chemists. Both suffered from the authoritarian and sometimes tyrannical attitudes of their bosses. In the shop world there was no union to support employees and no management structure which effectively supervised first-line managers. This was the negative side of the small-scale, family atmosphere of shop life which Audrey experienced more than Jeanette.

Jeanette's ability, taking on financial responsibility at Brough's seems to have been entirely taken for granted from the moment when, in a haphazard way, "someone decided" she should go into the office. Once her abilities were made clear, no one suggested that she take night classes in bookkeeping or seek other jobs using her skills. This seems in line with what has already been noted: that the expectations of the women themselves and of all those with whom they were involved, were limited. At this time Jeanette was about to get married. No doubt it was assumed that she might give up full-time employment for ever and that, if she had a job, it would be of secondary importance to being a wife and mother. Any thought of developing her skills to build a career would not have occurred to anyone.

Perhaps because of having held such a responsible job at Brough's, Jeanette was not prepared to put up with the rudeness of the manageress who wouldn't use her name, nor with being insulted and unjustly suspected by the manager at the Co-op. She had the confidence to leave. Would she have done so in a climate where jobs were less easy to come by?

Jeanette had the advantage of being in an employees' market when she was a young woman. The Personnel Manager at Osram's was needing workers sufficiently for it to be worth his while to try to dispel her prejudices about factories. She could feel "I'll give it a try", knowing that if she did not like it she could get a job in a shop. In fact she stayed until her daughter was born and, apart from a shop job when her daughter was very small, all Jeanette's subsequent jobs were in factories. She had become what Audrey called "a factory girl".

Someone who would not say of herself that she became "a factory girl", was Joyce. Wartime conscription took her from working in a dairy at Tynemouth into working at Tyne Brand. She worked on the paste floor, putting lids on the tins of meat and fish paste and, on another floor, putting labels on tins. Joyce disliked working there for several reasons: "Firstly the smell. The fact that, you know, the smell gets into your skin. No matter how many times you washed, if you went out at nighttime and started to get warm, phew, you could smell it coming out of your hands and I didn't like that. I didn't like, really, the type of people I was working with. You know, when I was young, if you worked at Tyne Brand you were the lowest of the low, literally. A lot of them came from South Shields during the war and they were rough. But there were some nice people worked there, but I didn't enjoy it at all - largely it was the way they talked - not necessarily what they said but the way they talked, you know, very broad. That grates on me. Another thing I found difficult was having to wear clogs in the factory. Everybody had to wear clogs and I didn't like that. But it wasn't difficult work at all. You had to work hard but, I mean, that's fair enough."

Joyce ended up getting seriously ill and was off work for three years. She really wanted to work with children and succeeded in doing so. After working in the south as a nanny, she came home to Tyneside in the early 1950s to look after her mother. "I took a temporary job at Ronson's until I could get the kind of job that I wanted. I was there seven years until I saw an advert for working with mentally handicapped children. I got the job and stayed twenty three years."

Her time at Ronson's was much happier than at Tyne Brand: "because they were very selective in their staff. Everybody that worked at Ronson's at least had to be clean and they wouldn't take anybody who didn't care or didn't want to work and a lot of them were married women. They paid very well but, like all American firms, they wanted their pound of flesh. You really had to work from the moment you went in, to the moment you came out. You couldn't talk - well, if I ever did I was always caught. But

Women working at Osram Lamps on the Team Valley Industrial Estate in 1960. The factory surprised Jeanette by being clean and she preferred it to the shop jobs.

they were quite pleasant people to work with and for. It was when they started building these industrial estates."

The new industrial estates built after the war on Tyneside were specifically promoted by the government to introduce a greater diversity of jobs in an area dominated by heavy industry. These jobs in light engineering were suitable for women. The economy was recovering and the climate surrounding working women and especially married women was changing. Neither Joyce nor Jeanette had expected to work in a factory but both found themselves doing so. In this way they were, perhaps, typical of the post-war woman factory worker.

But perhaps the change was also an interior one. Prejudices about factory work and workers were dispelled for those who ventured into factory work and discovered the advantages in pay, working conditions and trade union influence. Brenda's tribute to factory workers is a fitting conclusion to this exploration of the conflicting pulls of shop and factory.

"I used to hear a lot of people, including me own uncle, who used to say. 'Oh you'll not like a factory. The people are horrible; they're coarse'. I mean I have heard, I mean I still hear it from people when you say you work in a factory. And I'll be honest with you, the time I had in the two shops - give me factory people any time. They're down-to-earth; they're not selfish; they're very kind. I just think they're a different type of people. I don't know how people can get the idea that factory lasses are coarse and horrible and vulgar and rude. All right, you might get the odd one or two but you cannot class a whole factory full of people because you've got one or two bad people. But I still prefer yet, factory people to shop people. It's amazing the amount of things they do to help things - charities - help different places and all that. You never find that going on in a shop. I find, as I say, that I was only in shops about 18 months, but I still prefer factory people. Even now, if Angus's shut down, I wouldn't go back into a shop."

Photo opposite: Workers at the plywood factory in Wallsend in 1946.

Chapter 4
Changing Jobs

This chapter will explore why the women either chose or were forced to change their jobs, looking at this from their own point of view. Their reasons for moving ranged from financial and family considerations, through issues of personal relationships and practical difficulties at work, to the stark ending of the job.

This personal experience was, however, taking place against an historical background. Factors influencing their personal decisions included: whether it was war or peacetime; the range of openings in the region available to women; the state of the job market; the legislation governing dismissal and redundancy payments currently in force; the power of trade unions in the particular workplace at the time.

Money

Like Audrey, who went to Wills for more money when she got engaged, Nancy moved from the clothing factory, where she had started work, to a factory making plywood. She went there in 1964 after one or two attempts to get a job at a bedding factory. "Every time I went up, the vacancies had gone... so I went to the plywood factory and I worked there and I hated it. It was like working outside in the street. There was cars, like trailer things, going around and it was dark and noisy and filthy and they put me on a really filthy job - spreader - the glue! I had to wear a mask. I had to wear boots, these wellies, and this overall right away down and this pinny on, and a mask for the dust off the wood. Sometimes the glue was different glue - and the smell! It was, like, catching huge pieces of wood and plying them together - two ply, three ply, four ply - like knitting all day!"

They fed it through the spreader then "a girl and me would catch it and turn it different ways, it all depended on the length, fling it, and another girl would catch it, put it down and make the plies up. Then, when we'd made so many we couldn't get any more on the load, we used to have a sit and wait for the men. We used to wait ages for the men 'cos they were right lazy. So if you worked hard for an hour to get your load, you could sit for half an hour waiting for them to come and shift it and put it in the press. And ha' yourself a cup of tea and things, sitting amongst all the dust and muck - and smoking. I mean I wasn't used to people just sitting and smoking on the job. I mean the woman that used to shove the wood through used to have a cigarette in her mouth all the time. I thought, 'they're a right lot here.' But I was making more money than me dad, who was working in the shipyards. Much more. Me dad couldn't believe it. He was making £12 and I was making nearly £15". After about three months of this, Nancy left "because I couldn't stand it".

"Good" Jobs and "Bad" Jobs

However, after a short spell in a knitwear factory, Nancy "heard there was someone leaving, retiring off the number three spreader. That was brown glue, which wasn't as bad as the white. So I went and asked George for the job back. He was quite dumbfounded and he says, 'Seeing as you've asked you can go'. I was quite happy on there because I knew the girls and they were nice, a nice set of girls, different altogether, and the woods weren't such big bits of wood to hump around. I was there till I got married in 1966 and then in the summer they decided to close the factory 'cos Formica had taken over."

"So that was the first time I was ever made redundant, and the only time I've ever been finished in a job. So me mam says, 'Well, have yourself a few weeks off'. But I was bored and the dole was offering us jobs at Haggies [the Rope Works] and at Tyne Brand, and I thought, 'I'm not that type of person', you know. So I went back sewing for a girl I knew at the cushion factory and I hated that. So I just stayed there a few weeks and I went back to Clays and I got on the nice nighties and things. The money had changed then. In fact everything had changed round, the piecework and everything and I loved it. And then I fell pregnant." So she left to have her first child.

Nancy clearly managed to survive, and even to enjoy, doing some pretty unpleasant jobs. But it was not easy to guess, before she told me, which she had liked and which she had not. For example, when she left the plywood factory and went to the knitwear factory, she liked it to start with and then her feelings changed. "I was making good money there and I liked it. Then they found out I could do the waistcoat pockets and I got the waistcoat pockets all the time. It was a much smaller firm, about twenty machinists, and you all had to take your turn and they just didn't take their turn". She decided to go back to the Plywood, which on the face of it, would have seemed a much more unpleasant option.

Relationships at Work

What people experience as boring work is not always easy to appreciate for someone not actually doing the job. In this case, presumably doing the waistcoat pockets was in some way a fiddly or tiresome job and perhaps did not pay well. But another very important theme which emerges in these accounts of settling into a work situation, is that of the extreme importance of making friends, of having easy relationships with fellow workers. Audrey felt that if she had made a friend she might have stayed at Wills; Nancy liked her second job in the plywood factory because she was working with girls she liked. Joyce enjoyed Ronson's more than Tyne Brand because of the people working there.

Job and Identity

Another important point, which Nancy's account brings out, is that although she had become a skilled machinist - 'a Marks & Spencer's girl' - through her first job, she did not think of herself as exclusively that. She tried for jobs in varied workplaces. This was on account of the relative wage levels and shows that women, who were skilled in a traditionally female industry like clothing, were paid at such low rates that unskilled work could sometimes pay better. Perhaps, at times, the same was true for skilled, time-served men: Nancy and her father were horrified to find she was earning more at the plywood than he was earning in the shipyard. But, on the whole, thanks to the power of the craft unions in negotiating wage rates, a skilled man would think of himself as a welder, turner, electrician etc and would seek a job in his trade in a way that Nancy and other women would not.

June's experience illustrates this. She left her job at the Co-op tailoring factory at Pelaw in 1949 to work at Reyrolle's (the well-known switchgear company). "It was me friend used to work in Pelaw with us. We were both in the sewing trade together. The money was very poor and the money was good at Reyrolle's. So me friend left. She got me coaxed six or seven month after 'cos she always had more money than I had. She'd say, 'You're a fool sticking this rag trade, June. You want to come in Reyrolle's' - 'cos, I mean, you could go and get an interview and get a start. It wasn't, 'Will I get in?' So I went and had an interview. I'd never been in that kind of trade before. But I liked sewing the best."

June worked in the Reyrolle factory in Hebburn in 1949 where the money was better than the clothing industry.

She was forced to leave because the oil gave her dermatitis. So she went back to the Co-op at Pelaw until her first child was born in 1958. In fact, she went back there five or six times as well as working a season in a hotel. She knew the bosses and the girls, although a lot of them left as time went on. She summed up her feelings by saying, "It seemed because that was my first job, that was the place that I belonged. I always felt I could go back there."

Julie also tried to move out of the clothing industry when she was eighteen in 1967. She tried to follow her sisters who had moved from clothing into the Morganite factory, "because of the money. They could make good money. I went for an interview when I was eighteen, same as they did. Now I didn't get the job. I don't know whether it was because of me long fingernails or what. I couldn't pick the little screws up." So she went back to clothing and remained in that trade.

The person who changed jobs most frequently was Sally. After completing her apprenticeship in printing and bookbinding, her first move was to De La Rue's in 1969. Her wage had been £12 a week after she came out of her time, but De La Rue's, where her sister worked, "were starting women on about £30 a week, which was marvellous money, you know. So everybody sort of dashed over there". The factory was on the Team Valley Industrial Estate. After "a strict interview", Sally got a job as a re-numberer of foreign bank notes. "You had to go into a training school for a few months to learn all the different types of numbers and the foreign letters. That was interesting in itself, but once you got on the factory floor you were in little cages. Every different department had different coloured overalls and they had cameras on one side of the wall looking down, examining you all the time."

"So every morning you were allocated your work and you had a little black book and you had maybe piles of a hundred notes where, when they've been printed, they've gone wrong... and you're sitting in the cage and you re-number them. If you spoil it, you've got to knock to be out of the cage, knock to get in to the other cage where they have unmarked money without numbers. Show them the thing. They take it off you. They take your name. It's a right clart - very high security. You used to get

Balmbra's bar, Newcastle, in 1964, where Sally enjoyed working as it allowed her to meet people. Below: The Team Valley Industrial Estate, in 1961, was home to many of the new industries that employed women.

paid on how many notes you numbered. Very, very primitive machines they were. It was like a little press. You put your own type in, your own numbers."

Different sections were allowed to go early on a rota, "so they had a chance of an early bus." "Well, they had the security guards outside at the gate, and on my early nights I always got searched, so I never got an early bus in all the time I worked there. So I don't know - I must have looked a right rogue, so I used to get searched all the time. So anyway, being a bit of a - what's the word for it? - anti-establishment type person - I got up one day off my machine and the cameras were facing us, and I did a tap dance! I walked over to the supervisor and said,' Right, I'm putting me notice in.'" Sally had been there just over a year. "So that was the end of that for all it was good money". She would have agreed with Audrey, who said of her time at Wills, "I found money isn't everything".

After this, Sally worked her way through all the printers in the centre of Newcastle. "I've been to that many printers, I really don't know in what order I've been to them. It wasn't because I didn't like the work, it was I just didn't like printing. So when I used to get bored, I used to think, 'Oh, I might as well see some more faces.' All you used to have to do was, if you didn't like the job: on the Thursday I would ring the union office up and say, 'Have you got any jobs going?' 'Can you start Monday?' And I used to put me notice in and leave on the Friday."

After a time she started to work in the evenings as a barmaid at Balmbra's Music Hall and stayed there longer than anywhere - five years. "So what I used to do was, leave the house at half past six in the morning. Me Mam never seen us till twelve o'clock at night because I used to work overtime till six o'clock." She used to walk up to Balmbra's where the manager used to leave her tea out for her and she used to open up. "I was young and I just

thoroughly enjoyed it because I wasn't one for going out, and I would never have met people really - apart from all the jobs I've had!"

Sally was married for a short time to a man she worked with at a printer's. When her marriage broke up she left the printer's and went to live on the other side of the river in a flat. She got a job at Waddington's on the Team Valley Industrial Estate. "That was the happiest job I ever had... you never had a chance to be bored." They made labels for Schweppes bottles and Heinz beans and Silvikrin. They had to inspect for faults and used to say of the Silvikrin girl, 'Oh, she's got scabby legs.' Another facet of this job which Sally liked, but which was also a reason for leaving, was working on a conveyor belt carrying paper from the warehouse. "As they were coming through they used to get varnished and they started to pile up at the other end you see. So nobody liked the job because of the smell of the varnish. Well, in other words it was like glue sniffing! I mean I wasn't actually going out to do it, but if I could get on that machine I used to volunteer, you know, because the smell was just absolutely magnificent! That was shift work: 6am - 2pm; 2pm - 10pm. So I used to like it. The girls were smashing." However, after a time, Sally decided to move down to Lincoln, where she found a job in a Smith's crisp factory.

Sally said from the beginning that she did not want to work in printing. This, combined with the easy availability of jobs, made it difficult for her to settle in any job in the early part of her career. The work was undemanding and not equal to her energies.

She explained her unexpected move to Lincoln by saying, "I just been down there once and I liked it. I felt there was nothing up here. I just felt life wasn't doing anything for us. It was just at a standstill and I was in a rut. So I just got on a train and moved down to Lincoln." This was a very unusual step for a young woman born and bred on Tyneside to take.

Rows at Work

At least one of the printing jobs Sally left was on account of a row with a forewoman. The forewoman "was always picking on this girl, this little timid girl, one-parent family, her father bringing her up, tiny little thing she was, little ginger girl". Sally, who was "really one for outspokenness" went to the girl's defence, "I got ahold of the forewoman. I was going to punch her. She never picked on her again, mind. But she made my life a misery, so that didn't last long."

But, on the whole, those who worked in factories and had conflicts with the management, did so in a context where they were supported by workmates or by the union. Therefore the conflicts were less likely to lead to someone leaving a job than in the more intimate setting of the shops. Conflicts such as those Jeanette had with her supervisors were difficult to resolve except by her resigning.

Audrey, in her account of working at Angus's as a part-timer (1961-65), described how conflicts with management and being moved to different departments, led to her leaving. "I always liked working at Angus's, although it was hard and you were tired. As a factory goes, it suited me and the money was good. I worked there for about four years part-time. Then it started to get a little bit slack and they started to put you in different departments. The only thing was the part-timer hadn't any rights there. The full-timers had all the rights. Maybe I could understand that. But the part-timers, if they wanted to move you five times in a day, you hadn't to say anything."

"The union didn't do anything for part-timers at all. I always remember one instance - it was a wonder I didn't get sacked! But we worked mornings and so many girls worked afternoons... Saturday morning was a big help to your wage when you were part-time. There were about six of w' worked in the morning and we found out that the afternoon girls were always being told on a Friday afternoon that they could work a Saturday morning, and we never got the chance." They suspected that this was because a relative of the supervisor was on the afternoon shift.

"So of course, the morning girls were complaining and complaining, mumbling on, you know. So I said, 'Well, it's our fault. We should see about it. There's no harm in asking'. It was no good going to the union because the union "didn't want to know about part-timers." It was decided that they would all confront the supervisor together. "Everybody was frightened of him because he was a horror and he didn't care what he said. He used the language, you know... So we all went, but no one was going to be spokeswoman, so of course I had to." He greeted them by saying gruffly, 'What do you want?' "I said, 'We just want to enquire why we aren't getting the chance of a Saturday morning.' Crikey, I never heard anything like it. He exploded. He started to wave his arms around and shout and bawl. So I thought, 'I'm not taking this. I don't take this at home.' So I said, 'If you don't mind, we've only come to ask a question and we'd like an answer.'" The supervisor stormed off and fetched the manager, a gentle older man. "He was a lovely fellow. He came out and said, 'Well, what's the matter girls?' So we told him. He said, 'Well, I know nothing about this', he says, 'I leave that to Mr -'. I says,'We're aware of that. We just want to know why we're not getting the chance.' So off he went and got the records out of the office and the records showed that there was certain girls getting more overtime. So, of course, that didn't get me into a good grace at all with [the supervisor]. But we did get the chance of a few more Saturday mornings. But then the work got poor again and they started to shift the part-timers and the place they would put you was the Flash."

Audrey disliked this because nobody would show her how to do the job. "They were so busy making money that they didn't want to know about you." She sat, on one occasion, for half an hour trying to take two parts apart with a skewer. "There must have been a way". The supervisor came down and only said, 'You're doing it the wrong way.' So I thought, 'I don't like this'. Anyway we were put back and forward into the Flash for about a month. And at the time me Mam and Dad had taken a little colliery shop over at the corner of the street... of course me Dad was a pitman at the pit. Me Mam took it over. She found it was getting too heavy for her. So at the time I wasn't very happy getting moved up to the Flash. So me Mam said, 'Well. why don't you come and help me? I'll give you what you're getting at Angus's, but of course, the hours would be a bit longer.' We split the day up. But then, of course, we had newspapers and we had to be there for half past six sometimes in the morning. So it was a longer day but it was just round the corner. And it would fit in better with me because [her son] was at school by then. So of course I put me notice in - but possibly if they hadn't been moving me around I would have stayed there."

The close interweaving of home and work-life comes out in this account. Audrey called her experience at home to her aid in her confrontation with the supervisor, thinking, "I'm not taking this. I don't take this at home". The two managers, in their different styles, dealt with the women in ways they would not have dealt with a group of men: the first tried to frighten them off from making a complaint by bluster and shouting; the second treated them as a father, or perhaps grandfather, with a group of unruly little girls. This second tactic was revealed in the soothing and slightly wheedling tone which Audrey suggested he used.

Even though Audrey got no support from the union she did have at least silent support from her workmates. Those who worked in domestic settings were in an even more isolated position than those who worked in shops.

Phyllis, as a fourteen year old maid-of-all-work in 1934, started work at 7am. She had to scrub the front steps as the first task of the day, light the kitchen range to provide hot shaving water for "the Master", and then make the breakfast. On one occasion the family used the dry sticks she had arranged for lighting the range, to light the drawing-room fire the night before. She was left with no kindling. This was too much for her and she ran home, only to be brought back by her mother. This might seem a trivial reason for trying to leave a job but the impression Phyllis gave of her experience was that this was the last straw in a situation where she was always physically tired and in which she felt powerless and exploited.

Pregnancy and Childcare

Of course a frequent reason for leaving a job was pregnancy. That was straightforward but the problems of trying to combine childcare with a job were complex and could lead to the women leaving jobs that they enjoyed. We will return to this issue.

Redundancy

As might be expected of workers in the north east, many of the job changes or losses that occurred to the women I talked with, came on account of redundancy. Of the twenty women I talked with, nine had been made redundant, sometimes more than once. As we have already heard, Nancy was made redundant in 1966 when the plywood factory closed as a result of a takeover. Vera was made redundant twice from light engineering companies: in 1954 she was made redundant after seven years; in 1968 the unit where she had worked for fourteen years transferred its operation back to the parent company in Coventry. Those made redundant from Angus's were: Mary in 1980 after sixteen years' service; Phyllis volunteered in 1977 to go instead of someone else after she had worked there for twenty years; Margaret went in 1980 after thirty years. In a sense she went voluntarily, because the lack of work in the factory was making life for her as a supervisor very difficult.

Margaret found coming to terms with unemployment far more difficult than she anticipated. Both Mary and Margaret eventually got jobs as hospital cleaners, hence Margaret's remark about the Juvenile Employment Service asking her in 1940: "if I'd like to be a domestic and I definitely said, 'No, emphatically, no!' But I've ended up that way!"

Those who worked in the clothing industry were liable to being made redundant because of the brief lives of clothing companies. We shall return to this issue later.

"All you used to have to do was, if you didn't like the job: on the Thursday I would ring the union office up and say, 'Have you got any jobs going?' 'Can you start Monday?' And I used to put me notice in and leave on the Friday."

Sally describes how jobs were easy to find during the 1960s.

Employment Changes in the Region

This account of the working lives of women on Tyneside is chiefly concerned with the experience of those who left school and underwent their formation as workers between 1945 and 1975. In that period unskilled jobs in industry were easy to come by for women so there was no great worry about finding another job if you wished to leave your present one. It was only the older women, who had experienced the job market before the second world war, and the youngest entering the labour market in the 1980s, who were concerned about getting a job at all. Indeed, the youngest fared worst because full-time jobs in industry were closing down. In the 1930s women could get full-time jobs of some kind. The spectre of unemployment, however, haunted those whose memories went back to that period. Phyllis, for example, giving in her notice at the sweet factory in 1956, had applied for a job at Angus's beforehand, "because the instinct of being out of a job was still there." This instinct may have been more on account of remembering the general climate when her father, like June's, was out of work for years, than on account of her own experience.

Photo opposite: Metal Box Company, Heaton, in 1956.

Chapter 5
Working in Engineering

As explained in the Introduction, my contact with the women I interviewed was through my work as an industrial chaplain. I visited George Angus from 1978-1990 and recorded the interviews with the women during the winter of 1983-84. Angus's was an oil seal factory, making seals for a wide range of applications from aircraft to medical equipment. The factory was on the Coast Road in Wallsend and, until the late 1960s, was a Tyneside family firm dating back to the eighteenth century.

Many of the older workers remembered the days when Colonel Angus was Chairman of the company and used to take a paternal interest in the place. When work was short he would arrange for workers to go to his farm in Northumberland where they hoed turnips and did other jobs, returning home with gifts of vegetables. The manager who ran the factory, Harry Joy, had started as an apprentice and rose to the management job. He therefore knew, at first hand, the problems of doing jobs. Although the stories about him make him sound a rough and ready and somewhat autocratic man, he was a popular figure, perhaps especially in retrospect.

Margaret described him in terms I heard often repeated: "He used to come down and talk to you as if you had lived next door to him for years... If you were outside having a social event, he didn't segregate himself. He walked around. He was a good manager, Harry Joy. I'm saying he was a good manager - he might not have been a good manager as to production, but he was more for the workers. I mean, he started when he was 14, served his time. He grew up practically with the men. He just used to talk to them as if they were mates".

The factory had moved in 1956 to the site on the Coast Road from its original site in Walker. Harry Joy kept pigs at the back of the new factory, fed on scraps from the canteen. Vegetables were also grown. A story was told to me of how an apprentice was set to build a pig sty. He had just laid a thick layer of mortar along a run of bricks when one of the pigs came and licked it up. The lad was terrified because he thought the pig would die and he would lose his job, the pigs being a major interest of Harry Joy's. Fortunately, the pig's digestion proved equal to the mortar!

In the late 1960s the firm was taken over by a multinational company and its management practices moved on. Brenda described how things had changed over the years she had worked there. She had started in 1959 when she was 17. "When I

The George Angus factory in Walker during the war before it moved to a new site on the Coast Road in 1956. Below, the new factory in the 1960s.

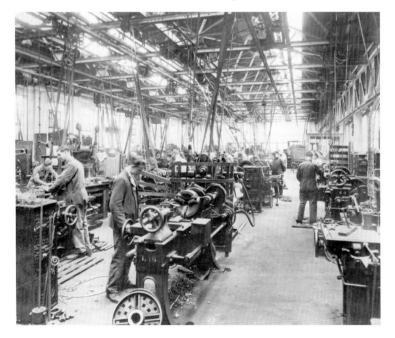

first went there, for the first few weeks, I didn't think I would stick it - not because of the job - it used to be the smell of the factory and the smell of the rubber. Now it doesn't bother us one bit. But I always remember the first few weeks. I thought, 'I'll never get used to the smell in here'". It made her feel sick. "It wasn't the job, the job was quite interesting - in fact I found it very interesting, but it was the smell at first and the heat. I couldn't get used to the heat."

I asked what had interested her. "Just all the types of products that were done on the job. I mean you worked in the Press Shop but in that week you could have probably about 80 or 90 different types of dies [moulds] in, and every one was different moulded. Some had two pieces, some had three, some were like a jigsaw puzzle fitted together. We used to make carbons. It was like, the black powder and a little paper doily thing where you used to put a load of soap in and make carbons like that.

"But obviously as the place expanded you couldn't cope with that type of handling. Now they've got the proper carbon presses. But it used to be very interesting because there was always something different. You had the same machine but all the dies an' that you got were all different."

At the time, women worked this section of presses on the day shift and men worked there at night. There were nine women whom Brenda found "very, very helpful. They were all friendly; there was no arguments. If you couldn't find something you just shouted across to your mate and she'd come round and help you and say, 'Well, that's wrong' or 'This is the way you should do it'. You got more help than you ever realised. I mean, they were on piecework then but they were still content to stop their own job and come and show you. It took a while, 'cos when you first started off, every time you got a new die it was different to something you'd had the day before and there was times you had to get up and go along to your mate and say, 'I've never worked this before. How do I do it?'"

The claim sheets for piecework payments were also highly complicated: "nothing like what they've got now. Then you used to have a sheet full of claims for: 'sticky blanks, blank separates, cutting cords, trimming cords'. There's none of that now, it's all in with the price of the job - cut to the exact size. But then it was an experience just writing out your worksheet.

"They were a close-knit group. I mean we used to have trips and everything in the Press Shop then. I used to organise a trip nearly every weekend, after a while. We used to go to different clubs. We used to write away and ask if it was all right to bring a busload. Actually, there's quite a few people at Angus's who are married now but they were single at the time and they just met through having trips. We never had any bother. Wherever we went to, we were always welcome back again. We had no trouble, no arguments, everybody behaved theirself. It was really smashing. Everybody had a great time. We used to have a collection a few weeks ahead. It used to work out about sixty pence each for the bus. The clubs used to put on cheese, biscuits, sandwiches. There used to be a dance band and that.

"Really, there's none of that now. The whole thing's changed and I think, when I think back to them days like then in Angus's, it was fantastic - the trips and the dances and that we used to have. The factory was smaller then of course. We had no new extension then. It was just one factory and you found that everybody just knew everybody. We used to have really good times. The outings to the clubs and that used to be good and now that's all just...." The trips ended, Brenda explained, when she was moved into a smaller department and could not continue to organise the trips for the Press Shop. I found it puzzling that no one had taken over the task. I suggested that perhaps the trips had filled a need at the time; if the factory had not been open long on its new site and a group of new, young workers had been taken on who were pleased to find an opportunity for meeting and courting through the trips. Brenda didn't think this explanation fitted. "I wouldn't say they were young people. I would say that out of the whole bus I was probably the youngest one. All the rest of them, in fact, I would say 99% of them would have been in the thirtyish to fortyish age group. There were very few young ones."

The success of the trips clearly owed a great deal to Brenda's powers of organisation. By the time I knew her she was one of the leading shop stewards and used her skills in that role. It would have been 1963 or so when the trips ended. By then, factory workers were becoming more affluent and more, like Phyllis, would have owned cars. The move began towards private outings rather than communal ones.

Brenda went from the large Press Shop into the small New Projects Department, just then being set up. "Although it was a small department it was a very close-knit department. You could do any job in that department. There was no grading like what you've got now. I often wonder if that was probably the best way, rather than the system we've got now. I think when everybody was more or less getting the same pay and just went from job to job you haven't got half the problems you've got now... You found that the press operators would even go and help one another then, you know, while now they haven't got time. They're just thinking about theirselves and their own money they're making. But I often wonder, we've got a wage structure now which to me I've never really agreed with it. I think there's too many big differences and too many big gaps between jobs and grades and B.S.I.s [British Standards Incentive] across the board. I mean it was different from the women to the men. But I think it was better then because everybody would muck in and get a job done."

The new wage structure was introduced in 1974. Brenda explained that this was in part prompted by the Equal Pay Act of 1970 which meant that women and men had to be paid equally for work of equal value. Brenda said, "Honestly since they've

made this new wage structure of ours, people's gone more miserable, more depressed. Every time there's a pay rise comes round we get into the arguments about the differential between the people in B grade and the people in G grade. The argument's always the same: 'why should they get more? My loaf of bread's the same', which is fair enough, but I think since we got the wage structure in, that's where I can see the change in the human side in our factory.

"People just haven't got time to lift their heads and speak to you or help you or anything now. Because they know when they're spending ten minutes or quarter of an hour with you, they're losing money for it... As I say, you could go through the Press Shop and they'd be singing and it used to be really good. Now they just haven't got time. Even the Christmas time and that, people had time to put up a few decorations and have their paper hats and make a little tree or something like that. They haven't got time."

Brenda was not alone in blaming the new wage structure for

Women working at the George Angus factory in Wallsend during the 1980s.

a change in the culture of the factory. I heard it from many people in my conversations, although it was usually expressed as "this place has never been the same since Latec's (the multinational company) took over". But people identified the wage structure as what had set one worker against another. Monica said, "It's the piecework. It's faster now with all the times being changed. You know, you got them in hours before and now everything's in minutes. You're just racing to beat the clock. That's probably how we're all tired as well. This structure that we are on now, this new wage structure, has changed every person in there. It's all money, you see. They're all watching what you're doing and you're watching what they're doing and one's frightened case somebody gets better than her. That is piecework I think. It was spoilt when they put the piecework on."

Phyllis described what happened when the new system was being introduced and she found herself becoming a shop steward: "Unions didn't interest me," she said. But she had had considerable experience as a supervisor in a sweet factory and when she saw what she considered a wrong policy being adopted in her department, she pointed this out. I asked her how she had become a shop steward. "Opening my big mouth! They were reorganising. They were negotiating a new method of pay. It was prior to the spell before it was supposed to be equal pay for women and men doing the same or similar work. They were negotiating a whole new wage structure. It was the grading system that they were on about - Grade A, C, D or whatever and this was prior to the thing being accepted".

Phyllis had been off work for seven weeks looking after her father. When she came back she found decisions had been made. "While I was away it had been negotiated and decided that the Cutting Room should be put into sections, you see. Prior to that, all right, there was scarfing, there was the air guillotines, the tube slicing, the benches, but there was no question of, 'Ee, love, will you help them out on there?' And people did it, you know. But they had decided to make it sections - this was for the grading system. So I said. 'Well, that's ridiculous'. 'That's what they've negotiated. It now will come in sections.' I said, 'Well, that's stupid. It really is. Why don't you keep it all one department, then you would all get the same grade and be interchangeable, the same way as you've always been?' 'It's sections!' - but of course much more dramatically expressed - 'Well,' I says, 'you're so silly'. So

Eva says, 'What do you mean?' So I says, 'Well, take you for instance, Eva. You've been here a lot of years and you've worked on the tube slicing but you're the last one to come on to these benches from the tube slicing.' She says, 'Yes'. I said, 'Well, supposing there's a pay-off - last in, first out. You're last in - the first one out.' 'Like hell!' (I mean Eva could swear!). I says, 'It's sections. That's how it would work.' 'Well, dear me, we must tell them! It wouldn't work.'"

As a result, the shop steward was besieged with complaints and decided to give up the role. Phyllis was asked to take it on and said, "Well, I don't want to but I've been shouting my mouth off... so I may as well put myself in the position to be shouted at." It was not a role she enjoyed. "I was never on a negotiating panel - I didn't fit in to that extent. In fact I didn't fit in at all. A fair way of thinking always got knocked back I found. One thing used to get my back straight up: when they were negotiating for an increase they always quoted the lowest paid and used that as a negotiating step. But as soon as there was money talked, on the table, and there was a chance that a labourer could take a 30/- rise and a press operator just get a £1 to sort of even the balance, no way would they have it.

"They wanted their differentials and they wanted them pro rata. To me it was wrong, because they weren't doing anything more for the money they were getting. It was purely cost of living that was demanding more money. Well, it didn't matter whether you were a labourer or a director, the cost of living affects you just the same. I used to say 'It should be across the board, a rise across the board. You've got your differentials in your grading."

There had always been a piecework system but, as we have heard, the new system was supposedly more scientific and evaluated "jobs" in a more detailed way. If the management hoped that it would eliminate disputes and ensure smooth running of the factory, they were to be disappointed. The new system increased the influence of shop stewards and the role of the unions because they were the negotiators.

In discussing how the unions grew in importance, Margaret, who was by then a supervisor, said, "It grew in importance because you worked hour for hour. Well, then they brought the piecework in and they were trying to push two hours' work into an hour's work, the management were. And the union stepped in, you see, and said, 'Oh no, we don't mind an hour and ten minutes but we're not going to have two hours'".

These accounts of working in an engineering works were dominated by what people said about how wages were determined. The women who worked there were working with men and both were represented by the General, Municipal & Boilermakers Union (GMB). This meant that their union representatives had more clout than those who represented the workers in factories, like clothing, with exclusively female workforces.

In Angus's the "skilled" men, who had served their time as apprentices and who worked in the Tool Room or as technicians, were represented by the Amalgamated Union of Engineering Workers (AUEW) which was more powerful again. But the combination of a skilled and unskilled male workforce, which outnumbered the women, meant that the women were in a privileged position in relation to most women factory workers.

If the incentive system increased the power of the unions, it also gave responsibility to the first line supervisors, who were responsible for sharing out the work to the workers in their departments. Audrey, who returned to working at Angus's after her time in the colliery shop, described what happened when the foreman was weak: "I came back to Angus's and I always remember coming in with one of the girls from the Inspection and she'd said,'Oh where are you going to work?' I said, 'Oh, Despatch'. 'Oh dear, you'll not like it there!' I said, 'Well, I worked there before.' 'Oh yes, but there's two kingpins in there now', she says, 'You'll not get any good jobs. There's two girls in there... and they rule the department. Nobody will go and work in there now.'"

When Audrey arrived, one of the "kingpins" said to her, "I don't know why you got started because I told [the foreman] we didn't need anybody. There's not enough work for us let alone another full-time." Audrey discovered how the "system" in the department worked: "The girls used to go and pick whatever job they wanted off the floor. I mean, the only department in the factory that was allowed to do that. And the poor operator, Jock, he - even if the job was in the middle of fifty stillages, he had to move all those stillages and get that job out. That was how stupid it was worked."

Caroline: "And what happened about orders that were waiting to be despatched, that were unpopular? Did they just get left?"

Audrey: "Didn't matter! They got left and you see the new ones [i.e. workers] that came on didn't know what they were picking. So you went down and just said, 'Well, I'll just have that', with the result you were getting the rubbish all the time and these two girls, their time was way up high. And, of course, the foreman, just did it for peace. He was too nice to be a boss as far as I was concerned." "There was an undertone because everybody knew it shouldn't be allowed."

After a time the two "kingpins" left: "and you know that department changed completely. The work was shared out evenly and no bother whatsoever... from then on the department just seemed as though everybody got friendly. There was no nastiness because the jobs were shared out fairly and instead of you going picking your jobs, they were brought to you by the service operator, which was correct."

Margaret, as a supervisor, took her responsibility for sharing out the work, very seriously, "I found when this piecework came in people were eating it, drinking it and sleeping it and I found it was getting to me. Because I was saying to myself, 'Now that person got treble time yesterday; that person didn't. I'll have to work it so it balances itself out'.

"They say that once you come out of work you should sever yourself, forget about it. But it's hard to put it out of your mind if you find you've slipped up and someone's been on a cushy job all day and you've got somebody on that hard job all day, which you usually split... Ye heavens! 'Cos you know for a fact, even if they're a good person to work with or to work for you, it's still in their minds. I used to be sitting alone on my own thinking, 'Well, I wouldn't like it myself, being mucked here and mucked there'".

The Role of the Union 'Appeals Rep'

A further refinement of the piecework system at Angus's was that the union had 'Appeals Reps' trained in the MTM2 system which evaluated the particular 'jobs' a worker did. When this system was introduced at Angus's the management put out an explanation for the workers. MTM2 was described as, "a way of measuring work without a stopwatch, timing by analysing the motion the person makes and applying times to these motions which are well established and recognised internationally. Where a machine or process time is involved, a stopwatch will be used as well".

Audrey was one of those who became an Appeals Rep. She had already taken on being Training Officer for her department and also its First Aid Officer. "And then they came and asked if I would go and sit a test to see if I could go on the Methods. I wasn't very keen to do that really because I felt as if I was getting older and couldn't be bothered with all these extra things. I had enough to come home to and cope with dinners and cleaning the house as well as going out. But, 'Oh well, just go and see how you come on.' But it was a job which worried us. I always felt as if I wasn't quite good enough for that. It might have just been because I was nervous but I didn't like to have to go and time people and think I was going to cut men's wages. I didn't like that. I did it but I was glad when it was finished."

"You see, although you were a union representative, there was no way that you could get round the Methods [Department's] times. You see, the men on the floor, the women on the floor, they would get a time off the Methods and they would say, 'Well, that's not good enough. I can't do that in that time.' So then they would send for the union rep to do a time on them to see if the time was fair. Well, I've never heard of anybody finding a better time than what the Methods gave. Because they - I mean - that was their job. There was no way that they were going to give a wrong time. So you were really doing a job that you didn't need to do. It was just from the top, for face, that you went and did it."

Audrey felt that what was needed was "a permanent union representative in Methods" rather than someone who did the job occasionally and was therefore not an expert.

To end this account of how working on piecework had an impact on the workers as people, we hear two descriptions:

The first is Sally, reflecting on why she preferred working at Angus's to her job in printing: "I like to be able to do something what I can see I'm doing, you know. I like to say, 'Oh, well, I can get 200 done now'. I don't know, I've always got to be working against myself, like piecework. I love piecework, 'cos you try to better yourself all the time. It makes the time fly over. You couldn't rush a book. If you rushed it you made a mess of it. Half the time, the printing side of it, you're just standing watching reams and reams of paper going through a machine. It was just boring. I wasn't seeing anything at the end of it, I mean. At the end of the night now, I can go down to the bottom of the

department and say, 'Well, I've done them'. I've always been the same. I just like to see that I am actually doing something... I race people all the time... I need a pacemaker. It wasn't trying to better anybody or get recognition. I need it for myself. I have to have a goal to aim for."

The second is Nancy, describing how the rhythm of piecework now informs her whole life: "You see, with us rushing all the time it's hard to unwind and slow down. Even when I'm busy doing my housework I think I'm on piecework. I can't just take my time doing the dishes, they've got to be done. I want things done before I start!" This might be an apt description of management's approach to production!

The Night Shift Issue

One of the ways in which women's and men's jobs were traditionally stratified at Angus's was that only men worked on the night shift. I had an unwitting influence on this practice coming to an end by setting up a meeting between women shop stewards from Wills and Angus's in 1980.

Women at Wills worked night shifts and their experience was positive enough to promote a move at Angus's to follow suit. The legislation in force before the Sex Discrimination Act of 1986 meant that factories wanting to employ women on night shift had to apply for a Special Exemption Order from the Health & Safety Executive. It was Brenda, as the most senior woman shop steward, who took on the task of persuading the management and the trade union to support the change. It was an uphill battle, "I never got backing off anybody. I was amazed. The only person I did was Jeanette. But, you see, I know a lot of people who don't agree with shift working and a lot of them say, 'I wouldn't let my wife come out and work shift work.' But there's a lot of men won't work shift work either... This is where I find you can't really take your union as an example 'cos they get on about saying that people shouldn't work shifts: 'it's bad for their health; it's bad for their digestive system - the sleeping habits and that change, and you can't get used to it. Everybody should do what they can to try to do away with shifts'. Yet, on the other hand, you've got new machinery coming in, which must be worked round the clock, and they tell you, 'you must go along with "technical innovation"', as they call it!".

Brenda's worry was that unless attitudes changed, women would be squeezed out of factory work, at least out of better-paying jobs. The particular innovation at Angus's which brought the issue to a head was that new machines had been introduced in one section of press work. These had to be worked constantly on a shift system. These machines were designed to do away with heavy work. They also did away with the removal of flash as a separate job (traditionally done by women) since the operator could now do this while waiting for the machine to complete its cycle.

Eventually the Exemption Order was approved. One of the first women to apply for permanent night shift was Sally. Her husband worked at Swan Hunter's Shipyard on permanent nights so, as she said, "it was like, 'never the twain shall meet'". However, things went wrong at the beginning... Sally went for a trial and was instructed by a woman doing the job to fit the springs with her fingers. They were supposed to be done with a tool. Sally wore the skin on her fingers so badly she couldn't do her own job for a week. The woman who instructed her had fingers that were so hard she could do the springs happily.

This experience nearly put Sally off, "and then, all of a sudden, I thought, 'Oh to hell, it cannot be that bad'. So, I've never had a sore finger. There was four of us: Millie didn't really want night shift (the older one we've got on night shift). She just didn't want to lose her job with her being a widow. She had put "day or night shift" in, so they hoyed her in between me and Mary as a chaperone. I would say that's the main reason why Millie got.... an older one to keep the other two subdued, I think. But I've always wanted it and eventually it was women's jobs they were taking away, see. There were so many women's jobs going to be lost"

I asked her: "What sort of reaction did you get off the lads?" Sally: "Terrible, absolutely terrible! They looked at you sheepishly... I don't know whether it was because they were watching their 'p's and q's'. Nobody spoke to you. The atmosphere - you could cut it with a knife. It's an awful thing to say, but one day, there was a group of them standing talking, and I jammed my finger or something and I let out such a swear word! And after that they were just great. And we've never looked back. We're just one of the lads now. I mean, they don't swear in front

Nancy, describing how the rhythm of piecework now informs her whole life.

of w' if you know what I mean, but we're just one of the lads. We're invited to all the bachelor parties and that, if there's a wedding going on. It was just that one swear word broke the ice. It was ridiculous!"

The strong opposition which Brenda experienced and the initial response of the men in the section when Sally and the other women were introduced into it point to several issues of important conflict. There was the sense of invasion felt when women were introduced into an all-male area, threatening their freedom to speak without constraint and offering a challenge to male power. They were probably worried that it would mean fewer jobs exclusively for men and that there was a danger that wages might be reduced.

Another issue hinted at in the remarks that 'I wouldn't let my wife come out and work shift work' and Sally's commenting that Millie was sent as a "chaperone, to keep the other two subdued", is the danger of sexual attraction between men and women workers. The opportunity for sexual activity in a largely deserted factory at night was clearly felt to be greater than in the daytime.

In Sally's story of her swear word which broke the ice and led to the women being accepted as 'one of the lads' we see some of the conflict being resolved with a fudge: treating the women as honorary men and inviting them to bachelor parties. This solution to the issue of sexuality in a group with one member of the opposite sex seems to have been a common one. A girl apprentice in a heavy engineering works used the same phrase of herself in talking to me, that she was "just one of the lads". I experienced the same feeling as a woman chaplain in a group of clergymen and a male social worker who worked in a group of women told me that he was treated as one of the women as far as their conversations were concerned. But that there was a tendency for the women to "look after" him when it came to drinks and food.

Although the world of work here described was forty years ago, these issues are still current.

Photo opposite: The Rising Sun Colliery, Wallsend, 1968.

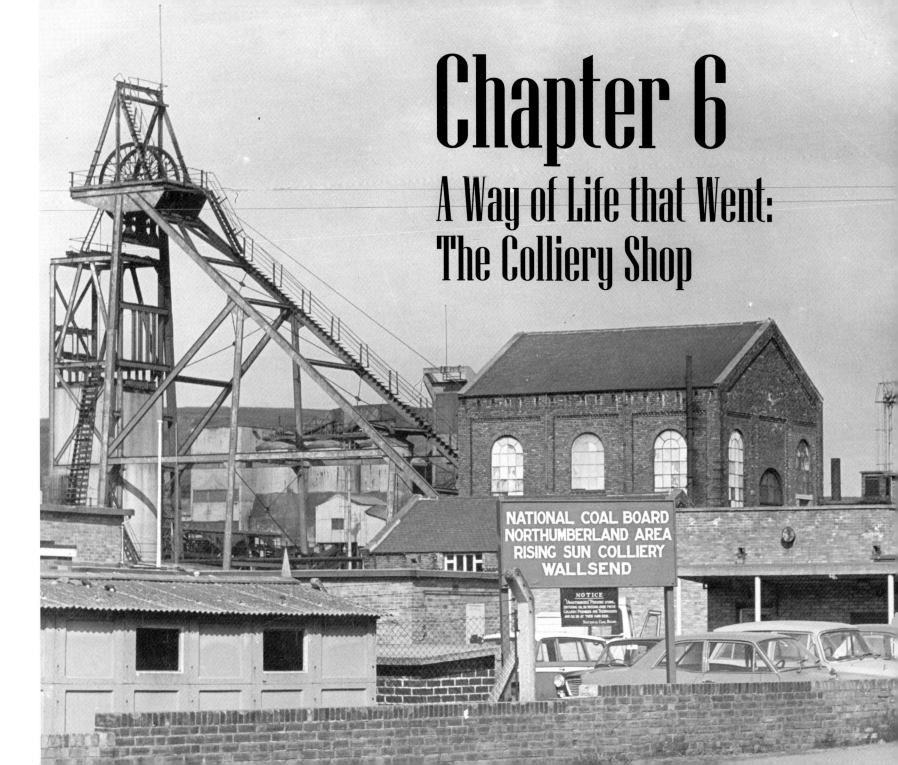

Chapter 6

A Way of Life that Went: The Colliery Shop

NATIONAL COAL BOARD
NORTHUMBERLAND AREA
RISING SUN COLLIERY
WALLSEND

Audrey left working part-time at Angus's when work was scarce, and she was moved round departments. She agreed to go to help her mother in the Colliery Shop serving the Rising Sun pit. She began by describing the impact going to work there had on her as a person.

"The new era of the Colliery Shop - that opened me out to a different person altogether. Because if the pitmen didn't change you, you just couldn't have coped. I was still quite shy. But you weren't shy after being in there six months because those pitmen didn't care what they said to you! They were great, honest they were. But I think my personality changed completely through them, because there were so many characters came in that shop."

"They used to come in for what they called their "baccy" and their snuff and of course then, that shop was run on tick. You had a big "tick book". But what bothered me was when I looked at this tick book. I mean, they used to come in from a Monday and pay on a Friday when they got their pay. They weren't normal-like names, like Frank Adams and Bill Coates. They weren't names like that. They were: 'Cotcher', 'Bandy', 'Young Limp'. Well, I said to my mother, 'How on earth do you recognise these people when they come in?' 'You know, it's just use'.

"Well, there was mebbe 600 men on that book from the colliery, and "Capstan F"; there would be "Young Tadger". I wished I had kept that book when I think about it. It was part of history. Another thing, when they came in they were always in a hurry. They came up for their shifts or they came out from the pit and they didn't want to wait. So you had to watch up the road and if you saw Young Tadger, say, coming, and you knew he smoked Woodbines, 20, so them 20 Woodbines were on there ready. And behind him was, mebbe, a fellow called Captain, and he smoked Players. So the 20 Players were on there ready - on top of the row of sweets.

"They came in and they didn't speak or anything, most times, coming home. They would just say 'Ta', 'Ta'. They didn't wait or didn't ask. Well, that was a lot to remember! You had that down in the book as soon as you'd put them on the sweets, you see. And honestly speaking, it was an experience! You had to be very, very, quick.

"Then at Christmas, it was the funniest part, because they used to... pitmen are funny men - they're not the kind of men that'll go in a shop and buy their wife anything. But they used to

come and ask us to do their Christmas shopping! They used to say,'I want a slip for my wife'. [Audrey imitated their gruff, embarrassed tone] 'Well, what size is she?' 'Well, a little bit bigger than you'. 'Well, what colour?' 'Oh, please yoursel. There's £5 - don't pay any more than that'. We used to have to go to the Wholesale and get whatever they wanted. And they used to come in: 'Oh, that'll dee. I divvent want to see it. Just wrap it up. Just get a bit paper. Write the card oot'. This was the kind of thing you did in that shop. Honest, it was great! It was great that shop. We really enjoyed it.

"I remember at Christmas, you had quite a lot to put up with off them as well. You had to be broadminded. At Christmas they all wanted to kiss you. It didn't matter if they were fifteen or ninety. That was the way it was! Well, as I say, I was a bit shy. But they didn't mean anything by it. They used to pay their bill and they used to shake your hand and kiss you - rough you know. Some of them had beards and everything and I used to hate that. I used to say to my mam, 'Will you come down?' And she used to say, 'Well, they don't mean anything.' And they didn't. It was just they were rough and that was their way of saying, 'Merry Christmas and a Happy New Year'.

"And they wanted to buy you a box of chocolates. I used to say, 'No, no, didn't want anything' But with some of them you had to, because if they'd had a drink... 'Oh, why no?' So we used to have to and they'd say, 'That big box up there' They used to give it and say, 'That's for you, pet. Happy Christmas!' Very, very, kind some of them. Of course, as well, if they were half-topped they wouldn't move out of the shop and you were waiting to get shut and you had to be diplomatic, you know"

Caroline: "It demanded a lot of different things, that job, didn't it?"

Audrey: "It opened me out no end. Definitely changed me from somebody that was... I never had much confidence. I was quiet and shy. It definitely opened me out. You had no choice. I mean, if you were in there on your own of a morning, there would be a shift come up at nine o'clock. They were all quite youngish blokes, between nineteen and twenty-five. You could see them coming down, five or six of them and you were going to get a ribbing. They used to come in and say, 'By, you're looking lovely this morning, pet! Fancy a date the night?' All this kind of thing - just "carry on". But I used to blush terrible, and of course they did

Miners on the last shift at the Rising Sun Colliery, Wallsend, on 18th July, 1969.

it because they knew I used to blush. So eventually I got used to it. It just stopped. It helped me no end, because I was always a little bit self-conscious an' that. But you hadn't to be with them. If you met them outside anywhere, you were a long-lost sister!"

"Then you used to get the odd one used to come on a Friday. Instead of coming in to pay their bill, would go straight into the pub in the field... and of course they'd come rolling past two hours later, you know, stick their head round the door, with their cap on, 'I'll see you next week, Mrs Johnson. I've spent a bit too much this week - all right hinny?' My mam always said, 'Oh yes, it's OK' They always paid. But that is the kind of shop it was. It was a friendly shop."

Caroline: "What happened... I mean there must have been the odd one that didn't pay, so what did you do about it?"

Audrey: "Oh, there was. Well, you see, they couldn't get past the shop. They had to pass the shop. There was no way they could get anywhere around it to get home... It was funny! You knew the ones that weren't going to pay because, as I say, from our door, of the shop, you could see right up the road to the pit. So it was the young ones usually that wouldn't pay. The older ones - if they couldn't pay - they'd come in and say, 'I'm hard up this week, can you wait?' And we used to say, 'Oh, yes', because we knew they would come back. But the young ones! You'd see a group of young ones coming down, and you knew the one in the middle wasn't going to pay, because you could see the other ones getting in front of him, you see! And there was a lamp post halfway down and they used to stand behind the lamp post, like this, thinking you couldn't see them! Of course, my mother was a character in herself, and she used to go out and say, 'It's all right, Willie or Tommy, or whoever it was. We can see you. If you're hard up just come in and say, and we'll wait till next week'. ' All right, Mrs Johnson, I'm sorry'.

"The only way you got involved with the wives, was if the men were off sick and the wives came up for their wages. They would come in to pay their bills and you got to know whose wife was who, but very few. You used to often get the younger wives up with their kiddies, to catch the men to take their pay off them before they went into the Club. So you met one or two of the younger ones and you realised which younger ones hadn't very good husbands, 'cos you could see them arguing on the corner, trying to get their money off them before they went in and spent it. You saw all the ways of lives.

"You also had the element of people coming up and borrowing money off you. They used to come up and say, 'I've got the electric bill in and my wife can't pay it. Can you help us till next week?' And of course we used to say, 'All right'. We used to lend them £5 or £2 and on the Friday when they got their pay they used to pay it back. So you were involved with their lives, you know. You used to help them out a bit and they were good customers to us in return."

"But we had some laughs - very, very kind people, the pitmen. Our Harry [Audrey's son], when he was younger, he used to sometimes come from school, come to the shop till I went home and, especially if it was pay day, every pitman came in, gave him a shilling, or a two shilling piece: 'There you are, son'. I've seen him go home with a pocketful of money. And I used to teach him not to take money, you know. Of course they'd say, 'Take no notice of her! Here, son, it's off me'. And they were all 'uncles'. He had hundreds of uncles.

"On Guy Fawkes... the kiddies in Queen's Road used to always bring a Guy up to our shop, because they knew the pitmen wouldn't pass them. Very, very kind - hard working and hard drinkers and rough, you know. I mean I've seen them go into the Club and come out of the Club and have a fight on the green and then shake hands and be friends again, But very, very kind people - salt of the earth, the pitmen.

"Some of them lived in Durham. Some of them were from pits that had closed down and they came in buses. Now, the busmen that brought them from all these little country places, used to come in the shop and have a cup of coffee. And of course all the people from the bus came into the shop, 'cos they knew the bus drivers were in. It was a little gold mine! I can remember that when my mam and dad bought it, they paid £1,000 just for the goodwill, and it was only a little wooden hut."

The close involvement with the pitmen and their lives of course extended to times of tragedy. There were three fatal accidents during the time that Audrey worked in the shop. The last was on the day the pit closed. One of the deputies was killed by a large stone falling on him.

"They worked in groups, these men, and the men had worked together for years, so they were like brothers... and the chap who was working with him - he came in our shop and actually my mother gave him a drink. He was in a terrible state. He had stood there when it happened, you know, and he was crying - we were all crying - because we knew him. That was the last day that the pit ever worked. You would think that that had had to happen. Another couple of hours and he would have been out of that pit for life. He'd worked there from he was fourteen. He'd be about fifty-two. And that was terrible. You felt as if you knew them, like your own family.

"What the custom was then, whatever bill was owed on that book was crossed off. That was the way it had always been in that shop. And when the widows or whoever came up to pay the bill, that bill was never taken off her. It was just one of them things that had happened, passed on from shopkeeper to shopkeeper."

The previous owner had made a lot of money. Unfortunately for Audrey's family, the pit closed in 1969, only two years after they took the shop on, and they lost money on it. Audrey tried to carry on the shop as a general dealers, but without the pitmen it didn't pay. "Nobody thought the pit would close. It was just a pity the pit closed, because it was a marvellous feeling in that shop. You couldn't describe it. It was just a way of life that went and it was very, very sad when it went".

This description of working in a colliery shop gives us a vivid sense of how the coal industry in the north east created communities and the culture of those communities. Work and community were interwoven in a very settled way of life. But this description also suggests how this was already beginning to break down - apparently unforeseen by those involved - "nobody thought the pit would close". Already other communities had lost their pits and the men were being bussed to this pit. For the present, however, the old ways continued: young men and sons followed older men and fathers into the pit; the expectation of getting a wage was secure, so the shop could lend without too great a risk. The discipline of getting the young men to pay up relied on the fact that everyone knew everyone, so the refusal to pay one week became part of an elaborate game - hiding behind lamp posts etc, of which everyone knew the rules.

The dangers of the work - three fatal accidents in two years in one local pit - explains the importance of making up quarrels between men who might be relying on one another for life and death when working underground. Williamson makes the point in describing work underground that "pitmen need to understand the precise roles of others, to know what to expect from other men, to learn that men can be trusted, and to acquire, as a matter of almost instinctive response, an ability and willingness to help others below ground. Without that, no pit can function."

Another passage in Williamson's book illuminates several aspects of Audrey's account, particularly her comments on the roughness of the miners and the fatalism expressed in her reflection on the accident on the last day of the pit's working: "You would think that that had had to happen." Describing the process of "pit hardening" he writes, "These attitudes include a strong attachment to the idea of being "tough", of not worrying about danger; they are extremely fatalistic attitudes which allow men to believe that they themselves are not really at risk, yet if they are to have an accident there is little they can do about it anyway. Then there is the value, central to their masculine self-image, of hard graft and a belief that only "real men" are capable of it."

Expressed in Audrey's account are some of the constant themes which have sustained the life and culture of the north east. These themes arose out of memories and perceptions of a past which was contrasted with the present: on the one hand people felt that the coherence and warmth of the old communities had been lost; on the other hand that the old times were times of deprivation and hardship.

Audrey remembered a community held together by the pit and whose way of life was determined by it. The roles of men and women were clearly distinct and the role of children was important. Boys represented the pitmen of the future on whose labour the community would depend. Perhaps what lay behind the gifts of the pitmen to children was the feeling that the brief years of childhood were to be enjoyed before the "shades of the prison house" caught up with them. There was also the hope that the next generation might achieve a better life and that son would not have to follow father down the pit.

It was a measure of how catastrophic was the collapse of job opportunities in the north east in the 1980s that the miners' strike of 1984-85 should have been on the issue of keeping pits open to preserve job opportunities and to keep alive the communities based on pits. The idea that a son might follow his father down the pit had become a hope rather than a fear; an opportunity rather than a life sentence.

The communities created by the coal industry in the north east had a particularly strong identity because they were small scale, based on relationships between the village and the pit. But other traditional industries also created what sociologists call "occupational communities" coterminous with social communities, whether complete towns like Consett, which grew up round the Iron Works, or sections within large conurbations, like Wallsend.

In the mid-1960s 29% of men living in Wallsend worked in shipbuilding, ship repair or marine engineering and nearly 50% of jobs in Wallsend were in these industries (Brown & Brennen 1970). Authors Brown and Brennen also found that over 80% of

This photo of Swan Hunter shipyard in 1970 shows the close proximity of the Wallsend community to its industry and employment.

the workers they surveyed in shipbuilding and manufacturing in Wallsend in the late sixties, "had spent their whole lives (except possibly for military service) on Tyneside, by any standards a very high proportion". They go on to make a point which relates to the sense of nostalgia for community expressed by Audrey. "One consequence of this absence of geographical mobility is that the majority of Wallsend's adult population have lived through and shared the deprivations of the pre-war years... Certainly our experience is that the Depression remains an influential memory to many who live in Wallsend, including some who did not experience it directly."

Brown and Brennen's study was published in 1970 before the spectre of recession returned. One of the things that depressed people about the 1980s recession was that they had thought that they had seen the end of large-scale unemployment and the blight to lives that it brings. People had brought up their children in the expectation that they would have a better life than they did. The generation who started work after the war perhaps did. But those who had children leaving school from the end of the seventies were worried about their chances of finding a job. Also, particularly if they worked in production industries, they were worried that they themselves might be made redundant.

The women in this study who had grown up in the 1930s certainly appreciated the post-war improvements in living standards. But they spoke with mixed feelings:

Margaret said, "Oh, it became a better way of life from coming out the Land Army. I felt as if I went up - I didn't have to scrimp and save, 'cos the money was coming in and I had a car and colour tele and telephone and all these sort of things which I thought were luxuries but now it's everyday life. Even people on social security have got that.... When I left Angus's - bearing in mind I was pleased to leave" (i.e. she took voluntary redundancy).

"But I felt so insecure in myself. It was all right for a couple of months. I was thoroughly enjoying - and suddenly this wave came over - and I felt so insecure I got rid of my colour tele, didn't I? 'Cos I was frightened I couldn't pay the licence. The car I got rid of; and I could've kept them all, but I felt so insecure."

Phyllis, whose family life in the thirties had centred on the chapel which she continued to attend, spoke about the social world after the war in the course of trying to explain her sense of separation from it and her separation from those she worked with at Angus's: "Their way of life was so different to mine outside the factory. Their talk was where they had been the night before, what club they had been to, or going to this dinner. Their lives used to be so different from mine. My life at that time was spent more or less going to work and coming home and looking after my father, and not going anywhere. But even if I didn't have that sort of responsibility of looking after my father, I don't think I would've still felt right and I don't know why. I think my way of life, or the way of life I had been used to, was entirely different... I mean a lot of them, like me, had known hard times but their outlook was, 'I'm going to make sure that I'm... all right Jack'. This sort of attitude. And, 'You're a long time dead. Enjoy yourself while you can'. But their way of enjoying themselves was different to mine so that I never really felt part of them. It's so difficult to explain! They got to know me at the finish. Well, you know what Angus's was like - suggestive drawings and this sort of thing being handed round the benches. They knew not to let me see them.

"It could have been that all that you earned went into the house and you were only given a small amount of pocket money so you didn't have the money available to do the things that they did, but I honestly think that had I have had plenty of money, I wouldn't have done the things they did. I like to be out. I used to walk a lot. I used to get down to the sea front or up in the parks... But the first time I got a car, then was a whole new existence! I paid £5 for it! That would be about 1958 or 59, something like that. It was a Standard Flying Twelve. Oh, dear me! I didn't have it many weeks and I sold it for £25 and used that as a deposit on a Ford Anglia. Oh, well, I was made then!" Both her parents were alive then and she used to take them out. "And I loved it."

Someone who observed north eastern life with an outsider's eye was Mary, who moved there from the south east in 1964. She remained single. "The pace is quicker up this way I find - the people, just going shopping, they always seem to be in a hurry, that sort of thing - where they didn't, they might now, down south - but they didn't beforehand. I think people up this area were more into factories. The housewife was working more up here than they were down south. Down south they were more or less part-time work - daily helps and things like that, whereas up here it was heavier, industry work and the pace was quicker and more tiring, of course. And they were having to fit the shopping in with their free time."

"I think women down south was more independent to me in a way. Up here, the wife, her place was in the home until the last so many years they've had to work and it's just coming gradually now that they're getting more independence. I found that the women was kept down more up here ... The women down south had more say in the house, I found that, fifty-fifty, whereas it wasn't up here when I first came. They had to do what their husband told them and that was it. I used to hear little bits and pieces... I found a big difference. I didn't say anything but I found out, oh, you were treated differently up here. But it's coming now. It's changing for them, for the better." I suggested that the fact that in some cases women had kept their jobs when the men had lost theirs had been an influence.

Mary: "Yes, the tables are turned now and whether the men can accept it all the way I don't know. Some of them are having to do the housework while their wives are out now. Some of them are lost completely, I think. The women are definitely having more to say now, which I think is a good thing".

These accounts give us a feel for how the changes that occurred in the post-war period were experienced by people living in the north east in ways which were both extremely personal and connected with wider social developments.

Photo opposite: Supervisor Mrs Cooper at the Elswick Works, Newcastle.

Chapter 7

Experience as Supervisors

Four of the women I talked with had been supervisors: Margaret was a supervisor for twenty-nine years at Angus's; Julie was a supervisor in clothing; Vera in light engineering and Phyllis in a sweet factory.

Phyllis at Field's

It was Phyllis who gave the most detailed account of her experience in the role. The saga of her time at Field's in the 1950s illustrates both the strengths of women supervisors and their vulnerability at the time. The principles she followed as a supervisor were those which the other women endorsed as good practice, whether they had been supervisors or not. These included: fairness towards those supervised, combined with sensitivity towards individuals; a pragmatic, rather than theoretical approach to the job and a commitment to straightforwardness in relationships, particularly with managers.

Immediately after the second world war, Phyllis worked as a van driver, having learned to drive in the army. Her sister worked at Field's sweet factory and Phyllis knew the head supervisor, Betty. "Betty arranged that I should go for an interview and I went for an interview with John Field and I got the job. It was just as simple as that! I started on the ordinary factory wages which was £3.9s which was almost £1 more than what I was getting driving the van." This was in 1949. The hours were 7.30 a.m. - 5 p.m. Monday to Friday. Saturday mornings were worked on overtime, mostly on cleaning the factory and machines thoroughly. "It was a very clean factory, Field's."

Phyllis was to be the supervisor in the Packing Department, where she was impressed by the deftness and speed with which the teams of young women packed the bags of 'Sixteen Favourites' by hand and, until heat-sealing came in, tied them with clips. At the beginning she had thirty young girls to supervise, though by the time she finished seven years later, there were sixty and two younger supervisors. This was Phyllis' first experience of factory work and I began by asking her if she was expected to train the girls.

"Well, there you see, I couldn't, which I thought was stupid. Not knowing the job, how could I show anyone if they were going wrong or anything? At first I couldn't, but new starters after that or new lines coming out, you know, or new packing designs, then yes, I made sure that I knew what I was doing before I put it on to what they called 'the benches'. But at first I felt surplus. I wasn't

going to stop there a week. Because after coming out of Faber's and having a full day and always being busy, I took very badly with just standing around watching. And of course the head supervisor, Betty, she was always busy. She did all the samples and apart from that she was sort of Personnel as well. I used to think, 'Well, I wish I could fill my time in like that.' But after a while - it didn't take really so very long - I got so that, well, I would mix sweets up if they were doing jars and what-not, and I got so that I filled the time in great."

This solution to the problem of 'standing around watching' would not have been open to Phyllis in a more highly unionised workplace. It was one of the problems which Margaret encountered at Angus's. She used to do a little discreet work on the benches if the industrial climate was not tense.

Phyllis felt that she had been appointed to this job because "they wanted an older person. They thought, perhaps, that the younger ones would respect an older person and take more notice of an older person. I mean, the girls on the packing at the time when I started, they ranged from fifteen years to about eighteen and at that time they were still just young - young girls.

"When I started I was just on a normal top-line factory wage, you know, age wise. You used to get a rise every birthday till you were twenty-one and then there was a ceiling. That was more or less the same all over. But after a while they decided I was OK and I decided, 'Oh well, yeah, I would stop.' Then I got a five shilling rise. It doesn't sound a lot but it was a lot and gradually I got more rises. You really had to ask, you know."

Phyllis chose the time to ask "when it was a busy time or when I thought, well, I was having a little bit more responsibility and a little bit more responsibility, you see. So eventually when we moved, when the Packing Department moved from the factory when they were sort of expanding, I was put in charge of that. We started more girls; began to get machinery in - I asked Mr Field what was in it for me. He said, 'Well, I've decided we'll put you on the staff and give you £7 a week.' Now Betty, at that time, she had £7 a week, so they rose Betty's wages to £10 a week. I was quite happy with £7 a week because I knew I would have that whether I was there or whether I wasn't - funny that though. When that happened I don't think I ever lost a day, you know. I didn't stop off even with heavy colds."

"Then the Packing Department grew and I gradually got one junior supervisor and then two. I tried to get extra for the girls on the end of what they called 'the teams', because she was more or less responsible for the other girls, spot checking, you know, heat-sealing, one thing and the other, but I never managed that. He was a funny chap. Actually he was a good boss in lots of ways. But like anyone else, he liked his pound of flesh.

"Of course there was no incentive at Field's, but you had a target to get out. Every week when I got the rota: two thousand boilings of such-and-such, all this. I got this sheet that had to be packed in that week and you had to really go at it. So you had to more or less work with them, you know, to let them see that you were working just as hard as they were. You had to - well, I felt I had to. I've always felt, 'Why are you asking someone to do something you can't do yourself?'"

Caroline: "So the incentive just worked from good will did it?"

Phyllis: "Oh yes. It did"

Caroline: "So how was that maintained by him? How did industrial relations work there? I mean you probably might not have thought of it in those terms."

Phyllis: "Well no, no we didn't. I mean, girls had off days when they were not so well. You just had to sort of tolerate that and maybe, 'I'll give you a spell at that for...' You had to - well, I felt as though I had to let them see that I was quite willing to make a go of it if they were. And it was amazing - they were a great bunch of girls, really.

"And, of course, John Field sometimes lost his blob you know. He used to park his car at the bottom, come through the warehouse and come through the Packing Department... And if there was a sweet on the floor, he would see it. Passing a stillage full of 7lb jars, 6lb jars, 4lb jars - if there was a sweet half wrapped - John Field would spot it. He was a hard taskmaster - the labels on the jar, no way could there be one skew whiff or wrinkled. He knew presentation was salesmanship and if his jars looked just any old way, well, people wouldn't buy the sweets".

Phyllis' immediate manager was Jim Green. The first sign of impending trouble with him came one Christmas when things had been going well in the Packing Department for some time under her supervision. "They were bringing out Christmas novelties and I don't think Jim Green had a clue as to how to really set about doing these. There were some novelties that were like children's building bricks only they were boxes, with various sweets in the boxes. He didn't really have a clue as to how to set up a bench, so that we were doing these in the quickest way. Well, of course, you could only do it by a process of elimination, couldn't you? When I went in the office on the Monday morning for the targets for the rota, he said, 'By the way, you're on your own in there. I won't be coming in there.' I said, 'Oh well' (that suited me fine really). But the dainty jars and the Christmas packs and what not, we just worked them out - Betty and I - we just worked them out - 'Perhaps it might be better to do...' before we asked any girls to try them so at least I would have a little bit knowledge.

"And it went great guns. Mr Green never ever came in to see how we were getting on or what was happening - not while I was there. But the girls used to have half an hour for dinner and after the buzzer went they all dashed down to the canteen. It was a mad scramble - half an hour wasn't long. But once or twice when I'd been a bit later going down, if I was in the middle of doing something before I went down, I could see Mr Green come in, just stand by the office and stand smoking his pencil and having a look - saw me and he would go out again. He never came while I was there. He would have a potter round probably when I wasn't there, or after we went home at night time. I don't know. But I managed better without him".

Later on there came a period when work was slack and six girls were to be made redundant. Jim Green called Phyllis into the office to ask for help with this. "Well naturally I thought, the last ones who were in should be the first ones to go, because to me they were all worth their salt. But there was one particular girl that must have been a bee in his bonnet."

As it turned out he had confused the name of the girl he wanted to sack and refused to believe Phyllis when she tried to convince him of this. "But this was Jim Green. He wasn't a manager really. He was actually a sugar boiler." [He had come from another factory]. "But he eventually became factory manager, but he didn't have it in him really."

But after that Christmas - I don't know if he was secretly hoping that we would get into a tangle - but he got more and more off-hand." A lad, Bobby, who worked in the warehouse and who had been an errand boy at the Co-op and brought Phyllis' mother's groceries, began to make his presence felt. "He was a canny enough lad. But Mr Green was always sending for him and he seemed as if he was spending more time in the Packing Department." One of Phyllis' duties was wheeling the stillages of packed boxes down to the warehouse. "Well, it got that, 'Oh, I'll take that for you', you know, and, 'How do you do that?' and 'What's that for?'. I would just say, 'Well, these are export'. Export sweets have special flavourings, special colours and what not. You did things a little bit differently for export. And I thought he was just interested. Well, anyone who's interested, you're quite willing to talk to them. I don't think he really realised at first because I can't think it or that he wouldn't have told me what was happening, this young lad. He was a canny lad.

"Anyhow on a Friday, he told me on a Friday, that he was coming in, you know, that he was having a white coat. And I said, 'Oh, that's news to me. What am I doing?' He said, 'Oh you'll be in an' all.' I said, 'Bobby, no way can there be two bosses, conflicting ideas, conflicting opinions. It wouldn't work.' And I says, 'I could no more work under you - now I know why you've been so interested in the Packing! Why didn't you tell me?' He says, 'I didn't know at first. Mr Green has just told me to spend a bit more time in the Packing.'

"So I went through to him, Jim Green, and I went barging into his office. You know I hate underhandedness. And I asked him. He says, 'Oh yes, he's coming in on Monday and he's going to be in charge.' I says, 'Oh very nice! What am I going to do?' He says, 'Oh well, you'll be there to help' I says, 'I won't! You can take my notice!'

"John Field, the boss, was away then or otherwise I'd have gone straight through to him. But Alan Field was there. So when I saw Alan come in I thought, 'I'll give him five or ten minutes and I'll go in and see him' (which was another thing that was nice about the place. You could knock on their door and if it was convenient, they would see you. There was no making an appointment or anything like that)." "So I went in and said, 'Mr Alan - 'Mr Alan' - that was what we used to call him - have you any fault to find in the work I'm doing?' 'Not at all, Phyllis, not so far as I know.' 'Am I doing the samples all right?' 'Of course.' 'Are there any complaints about the way I'm tackling the work at all?' 'Not to my knowledge.' 'Why is Bobby coming in charge on Monday?' I says. 'Why is he being put in charge over the top of my head?' He says, 'That's news to me. As far as I'm concerned

you're the supervisor in the Packing Department.' I says, 'Well, that's good enough for me.'"

Phyllis went back to see Bobby. 'I've just been in to see Alan and he tells me that as far as he's concerned I'm -' It wasn't a question of being in charge. It was the underhanded way in which it was done, you know. 'Ee well. Phyllis, that's what Mr Green told me.' And right enough, on the Monday morning Bobby comes in with his white overall on and the girls are - 'What's Bobby doing?' 'Well', I says, ' he's in charge.' 'Bobby's in charge?' 'Yes'. So by this time I was up to here, and I was being awkward. If you asked me anything - 'You'd better ask Bobby.' But I was miserable. I was absolutely miserable. And at the finish I says to Betty,'Oh I'm going in; going to see Jim Green; going to give my notice in.' 'Oh,' she says, 'Phyllis don't. Think about it.' I says, 'Betty, no way will they treat me like they've tret you.' They just picked her brains and just stepped over the top of her. They did. But of course Betty was that very placid, gentle nature. I was more fiery then than what I am now. 'Oh,' she said, 'I don't know what I'll do if you leave.'

"So I was just going to go into Jim Green's office when he came round the bottom end into the Packing Department. And he's just standing looking and he says, 'Well, how's it going then?' I says, 'It's not going. What you asking me for? Why don't you ask Bobby? I'm not standing this', I says. 'You can take my notice.' He says, 'Hm'. I says, 'Well, now I'm giving you a week's notice.' (That was all you needed). 'Well,' he said, 'I'm sorry to hear that. I don't want to lose you.' I says, ' Well, you've gone the right way about losing me. I'm not going to stand treatment like that.'"

John Field was away till the Wednesday and Jim Green eventually told him about Phyllis' resignation on the Thursday. On the Friday when I was leaving, Jim Green didn't come in. He didn't come in at all. And Betty was saying, 'John Field will send for you and ask you to stay.' I said, 'Well, he's leaving it a bit late.'" Eventually she was sent for at 4.45pm when the day ended at 5pm. John and Alan Field were there and another manager. John Field says, 'What are you leaving for?' I says, 'I haven't got a job. Bobby is apparently doing my job - why, I don't know. Master Alan said that as far as he knew I was still in charge of the Packing Department. He didn't know anything about it' And then, of course, John Field started to bluster and he said, 'You swore at me once.' And I said, 'Because you swore at me.'" [in a dispute

over mis-sized jars]. Phyllis continued. "'Just because I swore at you and you swore at me and one thing led to another. Have you been dissatisfied with the way I've been doing my job?' I says, 'I can hardly think so because you'd have had me on the carpet.' He said, 'No, but I had sort of...' (I could tell he was trying to think. I think it had been sprung on him). He says, 'I thought a good job for you would be sort of liaison between the Packing and the factory, you see.' So I said, 'No. You're just making a job for me'. He says, 'It would be a very good job, a very responsible job.' I said, 'No. You've left it until now to tell me about this job. My notice has been in for a whole week.' And of course he then said, 'Well, Mr Green hasn't really been satisfied with the way you've been doing.' I says, 'How does Mr Green know? He's never been in the Packing Department to query, to look, not while I've been there. And', I said, 'Of course he isn't here so I can't talk to him today. He isn't here.'

"Well, by this time the girls in the Packing Department outside were shouting, 'We want Phyllis. We want Phyllis.' And I said, 'I've given my notice in and as far as I'm concerned I'm finished tonight.' So he said, 'Look, think it over, over the weekend. Your job's here.' I said, 'I'll leave it like that but I know that I won't be coming back.' Because it was getting louder and louder" [the shouting outside] "and Betty was beginning to get worried. She hated raised voices and this sort of thing.

"Course, when I went out, here, they had a bouquet of flowers for me. They didn't know till the Wednesday or something that I was going to leave. I hadn't told them... I was as full as a gun, you know. They says, 'What you going for? Oh come back, come back!' I said, 'No, you'll manage all right with Bobby.' He was a canny enough lad, Bobby, he really was. But he wasn't the right type of lad for that job, he was too highly strung."

I asked Phyllis what she felt lay behind all that had happened. "I don't know whether he thought it might be better to have all men in charge. I don't really know." I asked, "Was it because you had stood up to him?" "Well, maybe so. But you see the way I looked at things, if I managed to complete a week's target and complete it correctly, satisfactorily, then I was doing my job. It wasn't always easy because often he would send word in - 'Marks & Spencer want so many boxes of Minted Gold' or something like that, which hadn't been planned for that day. You would set your machine up for another type of sweet, so it wasn't always easy. I thought if I got that with the girls - you couldn't do it without the girls - then I was doing my job satisfactorily and keeping the girls happy at the same time, keeping a happy atmosphere - I mean, hot weather... working in a hot factory, you know, getting towards 4pm and the girls were withering and it was hard going for them. I appreciated what they did."

Certain themes come out in Phyllis' account: first there is her desire to do a good job, to earn her money. She didn't want just to stand and watch. She appreciated the work of those she supervised - "to me they were all worth their salt". She did her best to further their interests, for example, by trying to get a pay rise for someone who had responsibility for checking others' work. She clearly saw herself as much closer to "the girls" than she did to the managers. Her method of drawing the best out of them was to work with them: "I've always felt, 'Why are you asking someone to do something you can't do yourself?'" The support that she and Betty gave one another was important. Perhaps the sense that the Packing Department was a female enclave made the male management uneasy.

Underlying Phyllis' experience in this job was her experience of the insecurity of life in North Shields in the thirties in which she grew up with an unemployed father. So she appreciated the security of being put on the staff with £7 a week regardless of whether she was there. Characteristically she was never off and would have hated to be thought to be taking advantage of the situation. Even when she left Field's in 1956 and jobs were easy to get, she said that in her last week she applied for a job at Angus's because she felt: "'I'd better get written somewhere'. Because the instinct of being out of a job was still there."

Her time at Field's spanned the period of post-war recovery. The factory was expanding and taking on new staff, buildings and machinery. Phyllis' account illustrates how the old "family firm" method of working was becoming unsuited to the scale of operations Field's had reached. It is clear that in the final conflict, the manager, Jim Green, had acted on his own authority in promoting Bobby and that the owners of the company were left covering up for their manager. The days were numbered when the production system and industrial relations could depend on good will and on the good example and personal relationship skills brought by Betty and Phyllis and, in a different way, the Field family. Shortly after Phyllis left, the factory was unionised. The men appointed to her job did not stay in it long. "The whole pattern of the place changed. Instead of going in for lots of 4oz packets and what not, they did more loose for shops like Littlewoods. They did big packs."

These changes reflected the rising expectations of the workforce at the time; the expansion of jobs for women with the development of the small industrial estates in North Shields and the changes in patterns of retailing as chain stores like Littlewoods and Woolworths opened sweet counters.

Julie and Supervising in the Clothing Industry

Julie became a supervisor when she was 19 in 1968. Like Phyllis and the other women she managed the role by staying close to those she supervised. She had been very unsure about taking on the role so young: "They thought I was capable, but I don't think I was at the time... She covered someone's maternity leave and when that ended Julie was asked to take over another line, which she did: "And then I thought I didn't like it. See, I don't know whether it was because it was all different girls or what, but you see sort of working with all the girls" [i.e. on her original line] "and then taking over as supervisor, I thought I sort of fitted in. I always had to fit, Caroline, if I thought I didn't I couldn't cope."

In the end a system evolved in which Julie took over as temporary supervisor when there was a vacancy. "It suited us because it was a change. But I didn't want it all the time." I asked her what sort of skills were needed for the job as opposed to being a machinist. "Well, you had to know every job, the whole job through. You had to sit down and show somebody how to do that job; how to cope with it if anything went wrong; and about their piece earnings. Me, as a member of staff, I shouldn't have been doing this, but I always did. I would say to the girls, 'You can do it a quicker way this way. You'll make more money.' I mean, I shouldn't have been doing that but it was the way I was. If there was a spare machine, I would get on it. I would do a few jobs for the girls and I would say, 'Here's the tickets. Yous get the money.' Because you were paid whether you worked or not."

Julie skilfully avoided antagonism from fellow workers arising from her position of authority and, by being a useful resource to the management, she avoided any accusation of over-identifying with those she supervised. The financial incentive for being a supervisor in the clothing trade was poor and good machinists, like Nancy, were loath to take on the role. Speaking in 1983 Nancy said, "You've got all the running around; take all the backwash; put up with all the stick off either side. It's all right if you get a good team. But you can get some awkward ones, contrary, and awkward and shouty at the least thing and not think for theirself. If you are on a good team it's OK, you get your work down, you get your work out, you get your bonus - 'cos there's loads of clauses against you for your bonus." For these and family reasons Nancy did not become a supervisor.

Margaret at Angus's

Margaret had 29 years of experience as a supervisor. She went to Angus's in 1949 at the age of 23, was made a supervisor eighteen months later and remained in the job until she was made redundant in 1980. She could remember four other women who had been chargewomen. In 1979 four of these, including Margaret, were in post. By 1982 there were none. As the factory contracted and departments were amalgamated, the women supervisors were squeezed out. This could partly be explained by the rule that the "unskilled", i.e. those who had not successfully served their time as apprentices, might not supervise "skilled" men. Women were automatically excluded because at the time they could not "serve their time".

There was also an assumption that no woman could be a supervisor in a department with a considerable number of men, even if these were "unskilled". When Margaret started as a supervisor, she had 70/80 women working on machines under her care. She would also have had a few "service operators" - men bringing in and carrying away boxes of work to and from the department and sweeping the floor. In effect Margaret would have been in charge of a section of a department, supervised by a foreman.

She had originally taken a temporary job at Angus's. After she was demobbed from the Land Army, where she had learned to drive lorries, she came back to Tyneside and got a job driving a lorry, but there was a three-month delay before she could start. She went with a friend, who was being interviewed for a job at Angus's, and ended up with a temporary job for herself. I asked her why she had stayed instead of going to what would have been a skilled job. "I think it was the mechanical part of it, the machines and that, you know, because I am interested in mechanical things - and then I just got interested in the work." The factory was close to home. Her mother, aunt and sisters all worked there and they were able to go home for lunch. Her mother said, "'You'd be a fool if you gave it up now when you've got a good job', which it was."

I commented that she must have made her mark to have been made a supervisor after so short a time. "I don't know about making the mark, but I was willing to do any machine, you see. When you worked in the Flash you weren't just a stoner, a grinder, which they segregated all them later on... You didn't know what job you were going on next morning till you went in and Mr Milton used to say, 'You're over there. You're on there'. So you didn't get sunk in one job. I went through them all."

Caroline: "When you were a supervisor, did that mean that you just organised the people doing the jobs or did you join in?"

Margaret: "You joined in; you done it all. You taught them, you joined in. You were a working supervisor then."

I asked Margaret about what effect the new incentive scheme had had on the workers when it was introduced. "Crippled people! Crippled people's minds because of the money - greed! Not being satisfied with, shall we say, £80 a week. They'd know they could make £100, so they would go for that £100 a week, knowing it's going to put somebody, who cannot make the £100, to be the first to be out. The management love that."

Caroline: "So it set individuals against each other?"

Margaret: "Of course. They just broke apart. They were killing theirselves. They were going out full blast from 7.30 till 4pm, not everybody but some of them, killing theirselves, just to get, shall we say, another £15 or £20 a week extra.... They're just robots. The latter end of them days up there, nobody had time to talk... They just didn't have time for anybody's troubles."

As we have heard, this meant that Margaret, as supervisor, had to be careful to share out the "good" and "bad" jobs equally. When I recorded my conversation with her, which was after she retired, Mary, who had worked in her department and was a friend, was also present. Margaret said, "I found I had Mary working for us - I'm not praising you mind! I found I had to put her on the worst jobs first. Everybody got their fair share but you had to be first. I don't know if it ever struck your mind or not? You were the first to go on that job because if not they'd have said, 'Ee, aye, they're mates.' You were always the first to be moved, just for the half day or the day, and then they followed suit. But had I gone the other way round, they'd have said, 'Oh, aye,' - for all they are good people".

As the work in the factory had run down, the supervisors had to keep a sharp eye out for any fiddling of piecework returns. Margaret said, 'Not being discriminating against the male sex, but they are more liable to cheat than women are. Women have this, 'Ee, no, I couldn't', where men have this, 'Oh, book it in. They'll never find it'. They're cute, and some get away with it a length of time and then they're caught. But it's very rare that I ever caught any of my women. I'm saying 'very rare'. I didn't. It was only one, but it didn't go any further and I made her work her hours. I didn't go to the management and say, 'She's cheated'. I worked it out between the girl and myself. She never did it again, you see. It might have been a genuine mistake but, there again, I just had to watch... She could have been snuffed out of the factory - like that! You've got to give a bit. There might be a reason as to why they're doing that."

Mary: "You always looked on that side."

Margaret: "You don't know how their mental - could have trouble at home and they need the money and they want the money, things like that. That was just an instance. I never found anybody there, deliberately shall we say, doing it on and on and on.

"When you're in the supervision capacity, you find you get to know. I got to know their very moods, their very ways. Oh, there's something wrong at home, you know. You got to know them personally."

Caroline: "Did the people that worked for you use you as a confidante?"

Margaret: "Oh yes. A lot of confidence was put into me and I can honestly say I never repeated. Probably the people who confided in us thought, 'Ee, I wonder if she ever said?' But I never did, not even to Mary, though we were close friends. Anne was the self and same way. You could tell Anne you'd committed murder and she'd never breathe. And for all the three of us were close, we never talked about work, did we?"

Mary: "No. Just if something big happened."

Anne was a highly respected and much-loved person at Angus's, not least because of the courageous way she faced successive operations for cancer over the years before her death in 1983.

Thinking about what Margaret and Mary were saying in this conversation and the underlying assumptions which seemed to be implied, I reflected that Margaret, Mary and Anne were all Roman Catholics. The value of confidentiality in pastoral care would have been an important part of their experience. The whole model of what authority should be and how a supervisor should behave, seemed to me to be rooted in their idea of priesthood.

The supervisor, in their view, was not in the job for personal advantage but as a pastor with responsibility both for the department as a whole and for the individuals who worked there. As with a congregation, or indeed a family, there is a fine balance to be kept between the needs of the group and the needs of the individual. In an industrial setting the added ingredient is the need for productivity and profit. Margaret, while being clear about her responsibilities to the company, was concerned, not so much about maximising output from her department, as making sure that each worker had an equal chance of making money.

Vera as a Supervisor

Finally, what was Vera's experience of being a supervisor? Unlike Phyllis, Julie and Margaret, who became supervisors early in their careers, Vera was in her late forties. After working in the torpedo factory during the war, she came back to North Shields and had two jobs in engineering works before being laid off, after seven and fourteen years respectively. The second time was in 1968. She was immediately offered a job in a small Ronson's factory making hair dryers.

"As it happened, we finished work on the Monday, started work on the Tuesday morning. So I was straight - I mean it doesn't happen now - but then things worked out well for me. We went training making these hair dryers. It turned out they wanted a chargehand. During the first month they must have been watching out and they decided I was the one so I got the chargehand's job. There was a chap above me and between the two of us we ran this hair dryer division at West Chirton." This was a new industrial estate. They had 54 women working for them and on the whole things went smoothly. "But you can get one or two girls in that 54 who can make life very, very unpleasant for you. But I got over that because I rather liked the job plus the fact, I was 47/48 years old and for me to be made supervisor, I felt a little bit chuffed about it."

Vera, like the other women who were supervisors, adopted a co-operative approach with those she managed. In discussing the role of trade unions she described how she had been involved in setting up what she felt to be a well-run union organisation at Ronson's. Vera's view of what this should be came from her experience in the engineering works where the unions were well organised and consulted their members in a systematic way. "The

Women workers at a sweet factory in the 1950s.

women at Ronson's had no idea. They must have been in a couple of factories where they had bad unions and I had to sort of... it was a funny position to be in because when you're a supervisor you're not union."

"But I was lucky in as much as a couple of girls I had worked with were with me at Ronson's and I suggested to these lasses that they put it to the new girls exactly how a union should be used. It worked out very, very well. If they had an argument, they would get their heads together. Then they would come and see me and it was only a final resort that the union was called in.

"Because we could discuss it among ourselves and I'd get in touch with Cramlington [Head Office]. I would discuss with my boss how far I could go and then I would put it back to the union, to the girls and I'd say. 'Well, that is what Cramlington says. Now it's up to you'. Then they used to bring the union in. But you got a fair crack of the whip on both management and the girls". By 'bringing the union in' Vera presumably meant bringing in the external union official.

Vera's aim, as a supervisor, was to establish a good working relationship with those she supervised. The world of Ronson's had more in common with the Angus's of Margaret's experience than the Field's of Phyllis's because there was a union and procedures to be followed. Nonetheless, all three would have said that their success as supervisors depended on their establishing a give-and-take between themselves and those they supervised. They occupied an 'in-between' role between management and shop floor workers which depended on their personal qualities.

As we heard in the account of Vera's life, she was offered the job of supervisor in the new factory at Cramlington. She would have dearly liked to accept but found that travelling on the bus made her sick. So, even though she was offered a house in Cramlington, she turned the job down. Her husband worked in the shipyard and was facing possible redundancy, but, as Vera said, " 'Ah, it's one thing me moving house for my husband's benefit. But, I says, 'no way. If he can keep his job in that shipyard, he's going to keep it and no way would he travel.' So of course I had to turn it down."

This incident was one of the most poignant described by the women I talked with. Here was a woman being offered a chance of exercising and developing her abilities in management, being thwarted by the traditional assumptions of Tyneside - that her husband's job, even if "dodgy", was more important than hers and that to move house on her account was out of the question. The importance of the shipyards in the culture of the area probably also influenced the situation. Had her husband worked in engineering, he might have been prepared to see if a job was available in Cramlington, but since he was a shipyard worker there was no chance of that.

It is easy, however, to be swept into a middle class feminist view and to assume that for Vera to have taken the offer of promotion and of going to live in a new town would have been a good idea and would have made for her and her husband's happiness. A move away from the close-knit community of North Shields with its shops, pubs and easy access to Newcastle and the coast to the new town of Cramlington with its mobile population of predominantly young families and its central shopping precinct, might not have suited Vera and her husband. They had no children and were in their early fifties. Also Vera, like Margaret, might have found that the industrial relations climate in a large factory in the seventies did not suit her.

In fact, soon after this period, Vera's mother, who lived close to them in North Shields, was needing an increasing amount of care. As would have been expected of her, Vera made this a priority and then nursed her until she died. To do this, Vera worked part-time at Angus's and split the money she earned with her neighbour who looked after her mother while she was at work. She then went back to work at Angus's full-time until she was given Job Release and left aged 59.

"Yes, the tables are turned now and whether the men can accept it all the way I don't know. Some of them are having to do the housework while their wives are out now. Some of them are lost completely, I think. The women are definitely having more to say now, which I think is a good thing."

Mary on women's changing role in the employment market.

Photo opposite: Women assembling radio sets at R.M. Electrics in Gateshead,

Chapter 8
Views on Management and Trade Unions

Phyllis, speaking of Jim Green, her manager at Field's, said "He wasn't a manager really. He was only a sugar boiler". "He eventually became a factory manager but he didn't have it in him really." The question is: what is "it"? What made a "good manager" in the eyes of Phyllis and the other women I talked with?

On the one hand, they respected the managers who had done the jobs on the shop floor and knew what the workers experienced; on the other hand, they were critical of those they felt were "jumped-up" managers who gave themselves airs.

One person who gave an example of this view was Julie, giving an account of her clash with a clothing factory manager with whom she had worked in another factory when he was a work study engineer. "I don't know. I used to get on with this lad so well. He'd changed so much I just couldn't stand him. I don't think people should change because of the position of their job. I hate snobbery and he, to me, talked down to me. Well, that annoyed me. He only lived round the corner."

In the old days he and Julie had played bowls together on the factory team, so she resented it when "He really talked down to me as if to say, 'You're a worker and I'm the boss'. I mean, I don't have to be like that with anybody 'cos if I've got a job I do my job and I pull my weight. He annoyed me. He really did. 'Well,' I thought, 'I'll see you, like.' I dug my heels in. I thought, 'I'll make him dance.'"

The manager most universally admired by those who had known him at Angus's, was Harry Joy. Margaret's account of him, already quoted, described how "he used to come down and talk to you as if you had lived next door to him for years. If you were outside, having a social event, he didn't segregate himself. He walked around. He was a good manager, Harry Joy. I'm saying he was a good manager. He might not have been a good manager as to production, but he was more for the workers. He started when he was 14, served his time. He grew up practically with the men."

Working in the Family Firm

Margaret's expectations of what a manager should be had been formed at the pottery where she worked before World War Two. "The management cared, personally. They appreciated them.... They shared their workers' troubles. There wasn't that class distinction. I mean, I've seen Len Dennis, he was the head one, managing director, and if someone wasn't feeling too well in the kilns or something, he would take his coat off and go in, not saying, 'Oh, we'll get someone else.'"

Len Dennis managed the pottery for the Maling family, who owned it, just as Harry Joy managed for the Angus family. The pottery, based in Newcastle since the eighteenth century, was a "family firm" both in being owned by a family and because whole families worked there. All Margaret's family worked there: both parents and five aunts. The only one who didn't was Margaret's sister, who was too young. "Angus's was like that. If I had a sister or brother leaving school I spoke for them and they just employed them."

This kind of family firm was a type of industrial organisation being gradually superseded in the period of the working experience of the women I talked with. Angus's became part of a mult-national company in the late sixties. Maling's did not and eventually closed in the sixties.

As we have heard from Phyllis, Field's began to make the transition from being a family firm while she was there and immediately afterwards when the trade unions became involved. Her description of her conflicts with management show the limitations of the family firm as an organisation, as opposed to the warm reminiscences of Margaret about Maling's. When people spoke positively of family firms (and it applied more widely than just to companies that were literally family firms) they stressed the family atmosphere and the sense of being known as a person. When they spoke negatively, it was to say that 'if your face fitted' you did all right. If it didn't you were exploited.

Such a system was linked with other traditional Tyneside practices: there had been companies that recruited either Catholic or Protestant workers; there was the custom of foremen at the shipyards recruiting casual labour from the men who "stood on the stones" at the gates, hoping to catch the foreman's eye. This method of recruiting gave foremen considerable power and they

Mailing factory, 1931

DO NOT MISS STAND Nos. 117/20, Avenue D,

where the making and decorating of the famous "MALING" productions are being demonstrated daily.

Merchants and Dealers are cordially invited to visit the Works, where a full range of Samples can be seen.

C. T. MALING & SONS,

FORD POTTERIES, NEWCASTLE-ON-TYNE.

Manufacturers of Earthenware of every description.

'Phone : 6193 & 6194 Central.   Telegrams or Cables : " Maling, Newcastle-on-Tyne."

could be suspicious of Employment Exchanges.

In 1934 the Newcastle on Tyne Employment Committee put out a memorandum to companies encouraging the use of Employment Exchanges. "It is difficult to overcome the opposition of foremen, who sometimes think that the Exchange will usurp their functions and their right of selection of labour. This view, however natural, is quite mistaken. All that an Exchange does, is to make a preliminary selection from among the workers on its books. These it submits to the employer or his foreman for their final selection. The final choice is entirely within their hands." (Newcastle Employment Committee, February 1934).

Such preliminary selection would have gone some way to preventing corruption and favouritism in the handing out of jobs by foremen. Other "informal" methods of obtaining jobs were through the network of societies such as the Masons, or Friendly Societies like the Buffaloes, which operated to help working-class

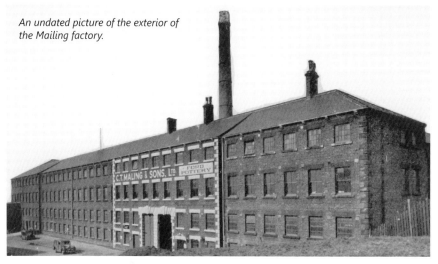
An undated picture of the exterior of the Mailing factory.

men "get a start" and to support their families in case of death or sickness. Women, of course, could not belong to these societies. They did not "stand on the stones". But they could be spoken for by relatives in the workplaces that employed female labour.

The Post-War Period

In the period after the war some of the women I talked with worked in the companies newly established in the area on industrial estates to replace the jobs being lost in the traditional heavy industries of the area. Hence the women worked at Osram, De La Rue, Ronson and Wills, where they described the strict regime and tight time-keeping that were the style of the time. As the post-war recovery got under way, the demand for labour increased and the power of the trade unions began to grow as the expectations of workers in terms of pay and conditions became greater. Various aspects of these developments were commented on by the women I talked with.

It was not until 1957 when Phyllis went to work at Angus's that she really became conscious of the presence of trade unions. As we have heard, in her time at Field's they had no influence. She had worked on the railways at the beginning of the Second World War and had belonged to a union but it had not really impinged on her. "The man in the power house" collected the union dues but that was all. "Because it was wartime, unions were furthest from people's minds". In Phyllis' opinion it was with the Labour Party's victory in the 1945 election that unions began to play a greater part.

Vera contrasted the conditions she had experienced on the Fish Quay in the thirties with post-war factory conditions: "When I first went in the factories, you started at 7.30 in the morning and your finishing time was 5.30pm. Now that whittled down to 7.30 to 4pm. Well, that made an awful big difference on your day. When you worked in factories you had proper toilet facilities which were a good thing; you had proper tea breaks which was something we'd never had on the Fish Quay. There you started at six on the morning. You got half an hour for your breakfast. To break again before dinner time, before twelve o'clock, was unheard of - but on an odd time, if it was exceptionally cold, the boss would let someone make a cup of tea. But you had to have it standing, so you can imagine a mug of tea in among the herring

and you were having your filthy hands! But when you went into the factory you had your hands washed and you sat down and you had your cup of tea and your cigarette.

"Oh, things changed enormously! And you started to have a little bit more say in factories. If you didn't like the way the foreman was treating you or something like that, you could go and complain either to management or union and something was done about it. But prior to that, on the Fish Quay, if you had a complaint to the boss he would say, 'Right, you're finished', and there was nothing you could do about it. You were finished."

June had her first spell of working at Pelaw Tailoring 1944-50: "I never used to interest myself in unions. I used to pay my union but I was never involved... It was just like going to work and doing your job and coming home." There was never any disputes ever when I worked at Pelaw. The only time that we kicked up - we used to have all glass roofs and on the top floor you got the blaze. We used to be always complaining about the heat and could they not put something on the roofs to - paint it or something. And then in the winter it used to be freezing... There were never any disputes about wages, like there is now."

Caroline: "And was anything done about the roof?"

June: "Why no! Na! We used to sit - well, some of the old women - when you're young you do laugh at older people. You think, 'What does she look like sitting there with that newspaper on her head?' But she made it like a funnel so it shaded the sun off her eyes for sewing and stopped the heat."

Joyce worked at a small Ronson's factory (of about 70 or 80 people) on an industrial estate in North Shields from 1952-59. She worked on packing flints and "service units" for cigarette lighters. These contained spare flints, little brushes and screwdrivers. These were part of the smart image of smoking being marketed at the time with expensive metal lighters run on lighter fuel. She contrasted her experience there with working at Tyne Brand during the war: "Ronson's wasn't bad, because they were very selective in their staff, very selective. Everybody that worked at Ronson's at least had to be clean and they wouldn't take anybody who didn't care or didn't want to work and a lot of them were married women.

"They paid very well but, like all American firms, they wanted their pound of flesh. You really had to work from the moment you went in to the moment you came out. You couldn't talk - well, if I ever did I was always caught. But they were quite pleasant people to work with and for." Not until after her time was a union involved.

The image of the pleasant factory employing respectable married women was very much the image that it was hoped the industrial estates would project. In the *Tyneside Official Industrial Handbook* for c.1950 (in Tyne & Wear Archives), the advantages of such estates are described: "Much has been done towards providing social amenities. Already playing fields have been laid down and, in a small way, recreation rooms have been provided and social clubs have been born. It is felt that a central social centre on most of the estates will have to be provided with a library, handicraft rooms, provision of proper changing rooms, space for indoor games and recreation. The trading estates must provide those amenities which large industrial corporations have already provided for their workers, but which the small industrialist coming to the area may find it difficult to provide out of his own resources." (p.133).

This vision of a Brave New Industrial World sits oddly with the accounts of those who actually worked in the new estates. Jeanette worked at Osram's in the Team Valley at the end of the fifties. By the end of her day she would not have been keen for any physical recreation. Strict control over toilet and tea breaks were maintained: "You couldn't go to the toilet. You just couldn't get up and go to the toilet. You had to ask someone to look after your work. It used to come along a belt to me and a girl used to see the solder was on the top of the - you know the two little marks on a bulb? She used to see if that was on. I used to have to say to her, 'I'm going to the toilet.' Now she used to put them in a skip and I had to catch up on them somehow during my day. So I couldn't stay at the toilet. There was no way... really. It was best if you didn't go to the toilet at all, because you couldn't bear to catch up on all these - sometimes it took you till next day, if you went to the toilet, to catch up! You know Angus's now? They would never put up with it."

"You got a break which was ten minutes in the morning and it went with a buzzer. And it was ten minutes. You had to go to the toilet then. I mean, they were so efficient at saving time in those days that there was a lady came round with a trolley. She put tea out and then the buzzer went. You always got your tea - it was cold when the buzzer went. You got it free. In the afternoon you got a cup of tea but you didn't stop. She gave it to you. Well, I mean, you didn't have time really to drink it."

When you say 'piecework' - in Angus's they don't know they're born! I mean, you literally worked from the minute you went in at half past seven, except for ten minutes and an hour for your dinner. You worked. You never lifted your head. You didn't know anybody because you never had time to speak to them, just in the canteen... but you only bought sandwiches. Didn't sell meals. But there was canteens on the trading estate that you could easily go to and have a nice meal cheap. And you finished at 5pm."

Another flaw in the idyllic vision of a trading estate as a centre for recreation and leisure activities was that they were deliberately sited away from residential areas. It is difficult to imagine workers returning in the evening, having finished at 5pm, for social clubs and handicrafts. Jeanette lived about five miles away. What she actually did when she left work was to call on her mother, who lived less than five minutes away from Jeanette. If Jeanette's husband was at work (he was on shifts) she would stay for her dinner with her mother. Otherwise she went home to get her husband's meal. The lack of shops on the Team Valley Estate and the lack of time for shopping, meant that she relied on her mother to buy anything she needed in the week and did her main shopping on Saturdays. In this way the old community life of Tyneside, centred on families, continued to predominate over the planners' vision of an industrial utopia.

When I asked Jeanette whether she had a woman supervisor at Osram's, she replied, "No, no, a man. Over us there was a chargeman, but he was all right. Nobody bothered really. Well, nobody had time to bother. And the girls did nothing. They didn't have time. Staff changed quick." While Jeanette worked there a woman in the Stores started a union. "And I actually joined. It was the first union I'd been in... and I paid my union till I left. Didn't do anything. I never knew why I paid it, but I did. I thought it was the right thing to do..." Jeanette's father was a miner, "and he was mad keen on the union and when I had been at all these other places, he used to say, 'Is there a union?' 'No, no, no, there's no union.' There was only about a couple of dozen in the union. Because, you see, they used to say, 'Well, what you paying that for? It doesn't do anything for you.' It didn't. But at least when we were at the factory, there was only twice I worked overtime there and at least you was paid." Jeanette was contrasting this with her experience in shops.

During her time at Osram's, Jeanette had an accident at work. There was no question of there being a union to demand compensation. What did happen was that one of the managers coaxed her through her fear and got her started on her job again.

Jeanette's job was to fit the glass bulbs over the filaments which then passed through a cylinder which sealed the bulbs, removing the oxygen. The other part of her job was inspecting the bulb for faults as they were test-lit on a moving belt. She had to wear goggles and to view the lit bulbs through a blue screen. This was just as well for, as she told the story: "This day it was hot and I was sitting doing this and, all of a sudden, I thought a bomb had dropped, because the noise was absolutely deafening. And I just sat and I was covered in glass and one of the cylinders had fallen." The bulbs on the belt were bursting as they reached it. "I don't know how many had burst before somebody had turned the machine off and I was, by this time, absolutely covered in hot glass. It was hot in there and I only had this thin blouse on and somebody had to take us to the First Aid: well, the noise in my ears! And I was all bandaged, all my arms and all my chest - I had burns all over. But you know they said, 'Well, if you had moved away!' I was so frightened I was rooted to the spot! Course I couldn't go back. There was no way on this earth I would have went back. They tried all kinds. I wouldn't go near I was so frightened. I cried."

And then, the next day, the manager come and he said, 'You're going to have to. Come on, sit with me. You know, it was a mistake. It'll never happen again.' And I went back with him at the finish and he put all the lights on for us for a morning." I expressed surprise that she had not had to be off work for a time after the accident. She replied, "No, I was OK really. Some of the burns weren't as bad. I was still bandaged the next day but I was sort of all right. I've never been a one for staying off."

Jeanette had said that the job at Osram's was "the best job I'd ever had." Looking back and describing her experience to me, it seemed as if she was describing a different working world from her current one. She said, "In Angus's they don't know they're born."

So far in this chapter we have heard about the women's experience of working in family firms and in the new post-war factories of the north east. In neither of these types of industrial organisation did trade unions, if they existed at all, have a significant role. We move on to hear about workplaces, particularly Angus's, where trade unions were important and where some of the women played a significant role within them.

Working in a Unionised Factory

Margaret, Phyllis and Vera all started work before the Second World War so they lived through a period of great transition during and after the war: the period of post-war reconstruction and on into the industrial relations world of the 1970s. They saw the rise of a professional management and, as a response, an increasingly professional trade unionism. They all had experience as supervisors. Vera and Phyllis had the experience of going back to being shop floor workers afterwards. Phyllis also became a shop steward.

They all shared the view that trade unions were important and necessary but they had ambivalence about the growth in the power of shop stewards. The industrial philosophy they held was that relations between management and unions should be conducted on a give and take basis. They accepted that, on the whole, management was well intentioned though ignorant of the realities of actually carrying out the jobs workers did. Unions were there as a kind of insurance policy against the exploitation of workers. They saw the shop steward as being one member of the workforce chosen to represent the rest rather than filling a role for which specialised training was necessary.

Brenda and Jeanette belonged to the generation which started work after 1950 and their early experience was, in many ways, of a different world from that of Margaret, Phyllis and Vera. They were both shop stewards but had not been supervisors and they tended to see the roles of management and unions as more formalised than the older group. Their experience as stewards was all of the world of an engineering works in the sixties and seventies. Familiarity with the details of the substantive agreement between the company and the unions and the implications of government legislation were necessary for their everyday work as stewards. They benefited from union training courses which increased their knowledge and confidence in acting as stewards in the male-dominated world of engineering.

Margaret went on from her appreciative comments about Harry Joy to reflect on her later experience. I asked her how it was that in large factories like Maling's and Angus's it had been possible to have an atmosphere where the employees felt they were known personally by the managers. Angus's, after all, employed over a thousand people. "Managers made theirself known to their workers, where I found later on in the years of working in engineering factories that they wanted that class distinction. They wanted to be known as that high and you that." (She gestured with her hands to make the point).

"Anybody in the management side then, they came from [the shop floor] and went up. They grew into their managerial position and they knew exactly what that person is going through. They have that compassion for that person, say doing a horrible job. They've done it and they know exactly how to talk to that person. Where you get these university managers - not that I'm against anyone with a university degree - and they haven't experienced it... They do the job in theory . They haven't done it in practice.

"You get these theoretical managers coming down and saying, 'I want it done this way.' And you know for a fact that it cannot be done that way but you do it that way to satisfy them. Then they find the other way was the best. So who do you argue with? You just do as you're told. This is what I found later on in my working life."

We went on to discuss trade unions. "I feel everybody should have a union. Because if there hadn't been unions formed, this present day and age, the manager still would have worn the white scarf and the dutch cap and the heavy boots, so as to kick! I'm not being malicious or anything... You've got to be unionised to stick together (unless you have someone who is a dictator and saying, 'I want it, never mind what my people want, I want'). The place would be in an awful state if we didn't have unions. I believe in them."

When the factory was on the original site women did not take a leading role in the unions. "The men led you," said Margaret. I asked if when the factory moved to its new site in 1956, the unions grew in importance? "It grew important, because you worked hour for hour and then they brought the piecework in and they were trying to push two hours' work into an hour's work, the management. And the union stepped in and said, ' Oh, no. We don't mind an hour and ten minutes but we're not going to

have two hours.' The union then was a good thing. It's still a good thing if it's led right. But you get them now, they're bombastic. They go to their management and say, 'But I want!' And the management say, 'But we haven't...' 'Yous are liars!' They won't listen."

Mary: "There's no trust is there?"

Margaret: "No. There's no trust now in the unions but there used to be. You had a man who was your leader and he spoke for you after meeting with you. But now they're speaking before they have a meeting and they're telling their force, 'We have said... Hands up!' And that's all it is. In my estimation a person on a union is just a spokesperson."

Caroline: "And when you say that, are you thinking particularly about your experience at Angus's or are you talking in general about what one gathers from newspapers and television and the general situation?"

Margaret: "I'm gathering it from some experience and some from newspapers."

This conversation was taking place in January 1984 during the run-up to the Miners' Strike which began later that year and when Arthur Scargill was much in the spotlight.

Very similar points were made by Vera. She harked back to her experience as a worker in The British Thomson-Houston. "We had a convenor who would never accept or turn down anything from the management till he first put it to his shop stewards to put it to the workers. Thereby we knew everything that was happening, even the slightest little thing. Even if they had, we'll say for argument's sake, decided to make a collection for some charity. The shop steward wouldn't dream of saying, 'Oh yes, I'll collect in my department.' It was a question of, 'Yes, I'll go and see my workers, see what they think and then we'll get back and discuss it.' That way we had a really good union."

This experience was what she judged her later experience at Angus's against when she felt there was a tendency for shop stewards to become "power happy". "Because they are shop stewards they think they're the bees knees and they're inclined to neglect the necessities that they are there to serve the worker, not the worker to serve them. They are there to represent the worker. I used to resent if our shop steward would go in and have a discussion with the foreman and it was signed, sealed and delivered in the office without it being discussed with the worker.

That was a beef that I always had. But, having said that, to me, a union, if they acted as they thought they should for the worker, they were a good thing. We certainly wouldn't have had the earlier finishes, when the finishing time was whittled down, that would never have been, without the union."

When Phyllis went to Angus's in 1957, a year after it moved to the new site, she found "relations within the factory were OK." Harry Joy was still the factory manager and he was "on first name terms with all the men and a lot of the women, who had come down with him" from the original site. "As regards union activity, well, there really wasn't any." Phyllis was on a wage of £5.7s.6d. "Then, after a while, I can't remember how long, we were told we were going to get, I think it was a three shilling rise that the union had negotiated. Then, after a while, there was another time when they'd negotiated, over three years, a five shilling rise and a five shilling rise the following year and then, supposedly, a big rise. But it didn't work out like that. It was after that time that the union sort of became more active, I think. Prior to that there really wasn't any."

I asked if the takeover of Angus's by the multinational company, Latec's, in 1968 had changed things. "Yes, it did really. The atmosphere wasn't the same. The place seemed to change: lots of new faces coming in and sort of taking over. Things just didn't seem to tick over the way they did before - not overnight, you know, Caroline. After a while Latec's policies crept in: 'Well no, that's not Latec's policy. They want this.' The unions, I suppose, were becoming more active. But I wasn't all that interested."

Nevertheless, because of "opening my big mouth", Phyllis got made shop steward at the time the 'New Wage Structure' was being negotiated. As we heard, she pointed out the shortcomings of dividing her department into "sections". Phyllis found the role an uneasy one. She felt that a lot of time was spent unnecessarily on protracted negotiations "and the whole purpose of being at work - to work and earn money - had been forgotten about. Work was less than secondary in the eyes of most of them. What they were going to get for nothing was uppermost, you know. And that used to rub me the wrong way - inwardly."

There followed a difficult period when, as Phyllis had foreseen, the issue of redundancies, or in this case, transfers, caused conflict. The manager sent for her "and said there was going to

be transfers and that five were going to be transferred. So I said, 'Oh, well that will be last in, first out then?' (That was the policy that the union and everyone had agreed, you see). He says, 'Yes. So it will be such-and-such and such-and-such and such-and-such.' I says, 'No. It won't. It'll be the last ones on the benches, not the last ones to start.' He says, 'No it won't.' I says. 'Yes it will. Your department's in sections now.'"

Caroline: "So you were making the same point to the management you'd made to the lasses before?"
Phyllis: "Yes. I explained to Mr Berry. He says, 'Well, that's fair enough then.'"

It fell to Phyllis to explain to her members what was to happen and the manager then spoke to those affected - by this time everyone had worked out who this would be. "It suited some of them. I mean, you can't suit everyone all the time." Her verdict on all this was: "They hadn't looked at it hard enough."

It is easy to see what a precarious position the shop steward was in when acting as go-between between the management and shopfloor workers. In fact Phyllis was sent to Coventry by her members at one point. This arose partly because of a problem with a manager and partly because she was absent from her department acting as a union representative on work study appeals. When problems arose, her members felt, "'Phyllis is never b... well here.'" The trouble with the manager was that, "You'd go and see him and he'd tell you one thing. So you'd go back and tell the girls, and then he would do the other. He would do something opposite. I didn't seem as if I was getting anywhere at all either with the management or the girls."

Eventually matters came to a head and Phyllis insisted on a meeting with the manager, the foreman, and some of the members. The manager's conflicting arrangements were exposed. Phyllis said to the manager, "This has been the trouble all along. You've been telling me things and then just changing them and you've caused a whole lot of trouble.' And I said to the girls, 'You see what I'm having to put up with?' 'Oh yes, we realise now.' But of course the damage had been done by then."

This account gives a clear picture of the transition from a paternalistic style of management to a style based on negotiated agreement between management and unions. Phyllis drew on her experience as a supervisor and knew what managing a department entailed, This manager imagined that he could negotiate with Phyllis and then instruct workers in the traditional manner. The result was explosive. Phyllis also observed how the new style made the workforce aware that they had power to improve their position. She felt this led to a scramble for money.

How the "Next Generation" of Shop Stewards Fared

Brenda became a shop steward in 1979 and later became assistant convenor, with responsibility throughout the factory. "At first I never thought very deeply. As long as the job I was doing was OK. I never really gave much thought to what the rest of the factory was doing. I can honestly say, since then, [becoming a steward] I know more people. I know about their jobs; I know when they're only fooling and saying to me they can't make money and they can - which at first I was taken in a lot of times with that."

"If they say, 'This job's disgusting. I'm not making it pay.' It's not the jobs - there's more things done by the management other than your bonus and your jobs. I'm more concerned with people being paid off, moving departments, moving people where they're not happy... That's a bigger injustice than they cannot make a job pay; or even the state of people's fingers and hands. They get good money and you find they get upset over trivial things and they don't bother with the things that are really affecting them."

She felt that her members relied on her too much. She gave as an example that when she had been away they had agreed to something she had warned them against. They complained to her and she said, "But I wasn't here!" She went on: "You know what they like? They like someone to blame and I don't think there's any glory in it." [Being a shop steward]. "Because I'm just there to get wrong off the Convenor; the manager; and off the women themselves... At times, Caroline, I get sick of being the one that everybody's got the right to tell off. And I think that's what I'm there for. It keeps the girls happy that they're telling me off. It keeps the manager happy because he's telling me what I should've done to them and, in the middle of it is the Convenor, who says, 'Well, you're to blame for letting it happen.'"

When I asked Jeanette what had been the good things about her union involvement she replied. "The good things is the people I've met when I've been away on courses. And the things I've learnt about other people... I mean we are tret like royalty compared with what some places are tret like." [i.e. in other workplaces]. She also valued her pastoral role: "The people you work with, they tend to tell you more, about, you know, 'Don't say anything, but...' And then they tell you about their parents or their children or about their husbands - 'Where can I ring up?' But they think you know everything about law; you're a mathematician. And you acquire these overnight, Caroline. It's not that you've been to any school. One day you're normal and the next day you're a mathematician, definitely; you're a marriage guidance counsellor; you're a policeman because you know all about fines and everything, going to court. Overnight you know everything! And if you don't know, I mean, they're very disappointed!"

This exchange came towards the end of our conversation in which Jeanette had told me about the very difficult time she had had as a single parent (including keeping this secret in order to get jobs). So I responded by saying, "But in many ways you do. I mean, you have a range of knowledge about all those things, haven't you? Some of it you've acquired because of your own experience, like the mathematician bit." (I was thinking of her experience of dealing with money when she worked at Brough's). "But I was thinking, listening to the story you've just told, that you seem to have acquired an education and a wide view of things and I'm wondering how that happened when you were having a life when there wasn't much space in it for one thing. How have you managed to have the wide vision do you think?"

Jeanette: "Well, I don't think I had any at first. I think it was because I had really to look after Amy [her daughter], not so much when my mother was alive and I thought all the world was against us then. I've always put loads of hours in at work. I'm never... I'm not cheeky. I couldn't go and shout at [the factory manager] and I always listen to what they say. And a lot of times, you see, I know what they're doing is right and I can't knock it. I can't find it within myself to criticise. Because somehow I know what they're doing, they're trying to put the factory right. I don't think I used to be like that."

What is striking about Jeanette's reply is that she put first and with great emphasis the deep influence that caring for Amy had had on her. She also made an instinctive connection between her commitment as a mother and her commitment as a worker. It is not surprising that, as a woman, she should so naturally have held together her personal and family world with the world of work. But we can imagine how surprising it would have been if a man had replied to a question about his vision of the world and involvement in trade unionism by saying that it was looking after his child that had been the most important influence. Even if he felt it, it is unlikely he would have said it.

In the chapter on the Women's Experience as Supervisors, I suggested that the role model of a supervisor assumed by Margaret and Mary was that of a priest. In what Brenda and Jeanette said about their roles as shop stewards, there are again echoes of the role of minister. Apart from their representative roles they describe collecting other functions: parent, scapegoat, knowledgeable on a wide front - all traditional elements in ministry. This raises an interesting question about what might be called the religious needs of people in a secular society. The roles once filled by ministers of religion may be taken on, often unconsciously, by others. Human needs find ways of being met. Those who become shop stewards or managers may take on the roles, as it were, at their industrial face value and then find themselves the focus of complex needs and interactions.

The conversation I was having with Brenda in the winter of 1983 was at a time of recession when the factory had been having successive waves of redundancies. At one point she said, "I'll be greatly surprised if Latec's keeps us open." What was being planned was how to vacate the extension to the factory and re-organise the departments in the older building. As she had worked in most departments in a wide variety of jobs she had a comprehensive view of what was going on. She spent a lot of time thinking about what would be best for the workers across the board: "We know the new extension's got to be shut and we've all got to be moved. Nobody's objecting to that. They can all see the logic of it. People just want to move with their jobs, with their work. And I know for a fact we'll have trouble in the Assembly over it. But I went home one night and spent nearly three hours on it."

"I started from the amount of operators we have; all the different types of machines we have and why you can't separate this'n from that'n. See, it's all right for the managers to say, 'Oh, we'll take the painter and we'll stick it there, 'cos we'll call this an "In Process Department"' - which is what they want to do. 'Now we'll stick so many machines in the Fabric'. But that's breaking up people's work practices that they've been doing for years and I don't think, I don't think really if it went to a Tribunal that they would get away with that - something that's been custom and practice for your job over years, that they can just chop little bits here and there and segregate it.

"I mean, for instance, the painter is part of the rota in our place where we do one day in five. Now they want to take it away, 'cos there's a new painter coming in, and just take an operator out of Assembly to work them painters. Nobody in Assembly wants to work the painters for forty hours. They don't mind working it for one day a week on a rota. But nobody wants to put up with the fumes and the mess and that for forty hours." Brenda went on to give other examples: "There's lots of jobs in there where they're physical and we'll probably do five hundred each per person on a rota and then we'll come off it. I spent a lot of time writing all this down. However, whether or not it's going to make any difference to the management at the end of the day, I've no idea.

Caroline: "I'd been wondering if there were going to be any preliminary discussions when the management asked for the union's view."

Brenda: "Well, they're supposed to before they shift anything but the way they're marking the floor and putting things on the floor, what machines is going where, it gives me the impression that it doesn't matter what I try to say, they're going to do it. And all I've told the members is that at the end of the day we'll just take them through procedure on it and claim custom and practice - that's been your job for twenty year... You bring a District Official in. He'll ask you, 'What are you willing to do about it?' And what they've said is they'll be quite willing to come out on strike. So I don't know whether they'll change their minds on that."

What comes over in what Brenda said here is not only the feeling that her careful thought about how the department should be organised may be ignored, but also the sense that she is describing the change in the industrial relations climate brought about partly by recession and partly by the policies of the government in the early 1980s. Much of her experience as a steward had been in the industrial relations climate, the beginnings of which were described by Vera and Phyllis. Brenda and Jeanette were accustomed to operating in a system where management sought approval from unions for moves they wished to make. Then, the threat of strike action would be potent. In what Brenda says we hear that that system is beginning to crumble. The union's power is undermined by the weak position of the factory as a whole. As Brenda said' "I'll be greatly surprised if Latec's keeps us open."

In Brenda's view, however, the problems were not just caused by the external climate. "It's definitely something within the place. I mean, we've lost orders and that but we've picked up a bit on a few orders … It's not working right. It's a multitude of things really. But one of the things that surprises me is that we've had that many changes in the managerial side: some of the people we've got in - I'm not saying - they're probably brighter than me - but at least I reckon I fairly well know the product from this factory from the Mill Room till it going out the door… We seem to have a lot of people in here, coming in now who still haven't got a clue what goes on in the factory and how many processes that product has to go through. I think they just think it's like making a tyre, where it's one commodity: something gets done to it there, it goes to the next place and it's finished. I think these people are living in Walt Disney land, because it doesn't happen that way."

Brenda gave an example of a mistaken management policy: the adoption of "cell units" in the factory, where all the stages of production would be carried out in one small area. Brenda had worked, years before, in the New Projects Department, set up on exactly these lines. It was found that work had to be sent out to other departments as backlogs built up; certain jobs didn't need some stages of the process so operators were left waiting for work. "The theory of it is that instead of it [the product] lying around from it being moulded till it's finished, which sometimes can be a gap of months.. It's supposed to stop that gap so the work'll come off the presses, get knifed, inspected, sprung, straight out the door.

"That is the principle behind it, so you've never got a build-up of work: it's coming in and going out. It's not happening. We've got some work from Department B now which is coming out into the Finishing areas… Now if people higher up don't know this and they're going into Department B and they're saying, 'Ee, mind, the work's going down smashing. There's no boxes in here like.' But they're not seeing the stillage loads that the bloke's

bringing out like - who's trying to justify what like?"

I commented that it seemed that the lessons learned in one five-year cycle got forgotten and had to be learned again. Brenda said, "You see, every Director we've had and every Works Manager we've had all come in with something bright. But it's always something that the other one said was 'nae good'. I mean an example is when one manager was here - 'We're only going to take large orders.' They wanted nothing to do with small orders. It caused headaches and there was no value in it at the end of the day. They were going to write to customers and say if they couldn't order a large batch they more or less didn't want to know … Then he left and we've got another manager. Now we've got to take any order that comes in to keep w' going. So if it wasn't profitable then to do it, why are we doing it now? Really I've never been so depressed and miserable as what I am at Angus's now. When I see half the rubbish that's being turned out, which the operators themselves know is no good, and you're told to run it. And you keep seeing stuff coming back and back for rectification."

Perhaps not surprisingly, in view of what Brenda said, her mother regrets Brenda's union involvement. "My mam just says, 'You should chuck it. You're going greyer and greyer. You worry too much. You bring your problems home with you.' Brenda, however, said, "I don't think I could give it up, because I like … I enjoy being a shop steward. It gets you down sometimes, like. But I don't think I could give it up because I believe in Trade Unionism." "I don't think it does you any good, like, at the end of the day. I don't mean from the workers' point of view. I mean I've been told by the management that I'm a right pain in the neck to them!"

Reflecting on what Brenda had said, I felt that her role as steward was the only one open to her that gave scope for her obvious management abilities. Even had she wished to do so there would have been no way for a woman of her generation and situation to have moved up the management tree.

Trade Union Education

What helped Brenda and Jeanette to sustain the stresses of being shop stewards, to develop their confidence and their ability to think systematically about the issues facing them, was going on Trade Union Training Courses. What they learned, particularly on residential courses, they found valuable. They enjoyed meeting one of the lecturers, a woman who came originally from Tyneside. She shared much of their background and gave them confidence. Brenda said of the training, "I found it very beneficial. The thing I liked about it is they kept you in groups. You weren't stood out on your neck on your own, like, worrying all the time. You were in a group of people."

Jeanette's view was: "While you're there you think, 'I've learnt nothing.' But when you come home and you think - you have. The very fact that they get you thinking about things. They get you up to speak. They let you say what you think without everybody laughing at you. You're encouraged to say your own thing, what you believe in. Whether it's right or not doesn't matter, you can say it to them. You learn a lot. You learn about the law. You learn a lot of bits that you think, 'Ee, I never knew that happened'"

Jeanette gave examples of the working of Parliament and of the Labour Party. "You learn about the structure of the union. I hadn't ever thought of things like that. I never thought of the money we'd paid, where it went to. You learn a lot about people; how people work and the conditions they work under. You also have to tell them something about your place of work and what goes on there, which makes you think about what happens at your place. Because I'm so used with what goes on... Angus's is a very unionised factory."

In this chapter we have heard, filtering through what the women said about their experience, an account of the development of industrial relations on Tyneside from the period just after the Second World War to the beginning of the 1980s. We have heard of the influence of different styles of management: paternalistic, scientific and remote, management by negotiation. It describes the growth of workers' influence and the beginning of its decline. Some of the changes were brought about by large scale factors: the state of the national economy, government legislation, technological development. Some of the influences were more personal: how authority was exercised in particular workplaces; relationships between individuals. Being a shop steward had an important impact on them personally and gave them, up to a point, an influential role.

"You've got to be unionised to stick together... The place would be in an awful state if we didn't have unions. I believe in them."

Margaret on the importance of trade unions.

Photo opposite: Traditional dressmaking in 1946 at the Tailoring Department of Blaylocks, Newcastle.

Chapter 9
The Clothing Industry

While the majority of the women I talked with worked at Angus's, the other workplace I visited was Louise Argyle, a workers' clothing co-operative in Hebburn, South Tyneside, which was set up in 1981. It began with a sit-in and much publicity. We will come to this dramatic story in the next chapter but first we will hear about the experience of those who worked in the clothing industry whom I met at Louise Argyle.

June had started at the Pelaw Co-op Tailoring factory in 1944. "It was no way like the rag trade is now [in 1983]. It wasn't racing to do - it was quality not quantity." When I worked first at Pelaw there used to be cloth and jackets and suits made and just piled up on the sides all round the factories. They used to get knocked over when people used to run home finishing when the bell went. We'd get the job next day of putting them all tidy. They'd lain there that long, we used to find nests of mice - with no skin on - newborn little baby mice amongst all these... That's how Speedy Gonzalez the rag trade was then."

She remembered that there were still "these cross-legged tailors - 'tinker tailors' we used to call them - used to sit cross-legged and they'd edge stitch round - in fact they'd made suits without any machining, all hand done. They started to dwindle away. They either left or there wasn't a job for them because this was the starting of the new way of sewing trade and there was no room for that kind of thing."

"They started bringing these belts in, the conveyor belts. You used to have big flat trays. They would put a job on each tray and there was a girl used to feed the belt, the Feeder. She used to put the whole jacket in their pieces: the backs, the fronts. Each girl sat at either side of the conveyor belt and as the trays came down you took your part of your job off. But what we used to do, we used to get crafty. We used to shove a couple of empty trays in between and split the work between three trays to make it look as if your tray had a job on. We got crafty!"

Angela Coyle in *Sex and Skill in the Organisation of the Clothing Industry* (1982) looks at how women's jobs in clothing were "de-skilled". Instead of making-up a whole garment ("making through") "most processes have now become mechanised, and each has been broken down into operations of the simplest form and the shortest time. The assembly of a garment is now based on a series of short simple operations for which operators can be trained very quickly ."

Despite this view, the women I talked with - who worked in clothing, regarded themselves as skilled workers, mostly dependent on their ability to work with accuracy at high speed. There was also an intangible quality connected with their relationship with material.

Julie remembered someone who interviewed her saying, "I knew you were a good machinist as soon as you picked the material up." Julie went on, "You know, you can tell, mind. When anybody comes for a job, you don't even have to watch them sew: it's how they handle the material and that."

The clothing trade consistently provided jobs for women in the north east during the period with which this book is concerned. But there was an increasing threat from overseas, for example from the Indian subcontinent, where labour was cheap and conditions not acceptable in Britain.

Sophisticated machines were introduced to keep the British trade competitive. Author Hardill (1985) highlighted the influence of Marks & Spencer who "insisted that its suppliers embark upon a policy of investing in new technology to hold down costs."

I asked Nancy about the machines she was using and the speed of work: "The machines are fantastic. I mean I was on a machine that back-tacked for you and everything. I don't like it. I don't mind the machines what cut off. That's what I'm on now. One of these automatics had me dizzy! He was having us on, saying, 'If you can use this machine you'll drive a car no bother!' But the other week the girl who was on the elasticating machine, she wasn't in, so I went up because there was a merchandiser coming. [The boss] said, 'Sit on this machine.' Because it's got eight big balls of elastic and all these needles and all these rollers and things. It's murder when you have to thread them all up. You have to use a special thread and things. I'm sitting there as though I'm - you know - this merchandiser come, to try and impress him with this machine. The machinery is fantastic."

Julie was asked by the manager, "who lived round the corner" and whom she had liked when they worked together in the past, to come to his factory to work on a recently acquired elasticator. "It had eight threads on it. It had four needles and four underneath threads. It was to elasticate the waists of these skirts. We were making these cheap skirts for Tesco's. And he didn't know anybody else who had worked one of these machines but me. Well, that annoyed me - all the girls he had in the factory -

and he didn't know anybody else who had worked a one of these machines before. I thought, 'You used me'

"This was in the light of what was to transpire. After trouble with the machine and its replacement and having the mechanic on it three, four, five, six times a day. I thought, 'Well, I'm not using it if it's not right'. Couldn't get the right sizes on the skirts. You can imagine - elastic - it's all right when it comes through the machine and it's moving down the line - but the skirts, it moves in - elastic. So you'd have to make them a bit big for them to finish off at their right size. I knew all this, but the manageress, just a young girl she was, I says, 'By the time they get down there, pet, they'll have shrunk.' She says, 'Do you reckon?' She must have thought, 'We've got a right one here'. I says, 'I'm not taking them back.' Because she wanted us to pick them all out. I says, 'You've got no chance.' So the next day she came and she measured them and sure enough they'd shrunk. 'Ee', she says, 'You were right!' 'Well,' I says. 'I know. I've worked a one of these before, remember? That's what I was brought here for.' So anyway, I got to like it a bit, this job. I got that I was doing 700 a day. And it wasn't enough. They wanted us to do 1200 a day. It was a physical impossibility."

I asked how the manager had arrived at this figure. "I couldn't tell you. But I used to go in at 8 o'clock on a morning, put my head down. And I thought, 'I'll show you! It cannot be done. It's an impossibility!' And I really worked this day. I mean, I worked every day but this day I thought, 'I'm really going to put meself out.' And I worked hard, really hard, and I think I done forty more than I would normally have done. I was shattered. We didn't finish till quarter to five. I never stopped the whole day."

The manageress brought the Work Study Engineer from one of their other factories. "He came and stood over us all day and I still didn't do any more. It took us ten minutes to change me threads 'cos I had eight threads on that machine. And I says, 'I hope you've taken all this into account, like'. 'Oh,' he says, 'I'm reckoning the time up.' I still couldn't do any more but they wanted me to do 1200, between 1200 and 1400 a day and it was just a physical impossibility."

I asked what the Work Study man had said, since it must have been obvious. "He says 'he's sure somebody else could do it quicker.' I mean, probably over weeks and months..."

Julie went to see the manager. "He says, 'Now we're in this office, just the two of w', I don't like your attitude at all.' I says, 'You've brought me here to make a mockery of me and you're not going to. I've slogged my guts out on that job,' I says, 'and it's a physical impossibility. You know as well as me there's not many people could do more than what I've done on that machine.' He says, 'I'm quite aware of that, Julie.' He knew. He was just trying me patience."

This exchange led to her walking out on the job. As we have seen, she was not the only one of the women who left jobs after rows with management. In this instance, Julie felt powerless to make her point in any other way. Her only power in the situation was her ability with the elasticator and while she could deprive the manager of that, she had no other power to change the situation. Had she worked at Angus's, for example, she could have appealed against the Work Study timings and the union would have checked the engineer's conclusions. It would have been discussed by the Appeals Panel made up of representatives of union and management and a verdict reached. No such machinery existed in a clothing factory where the union's power was weak. Managers in the clothing trade were men and had never worked on machines. No doubt in this case he had been given targets by his bosses and perhaps the suppliers of the elasticator had promised greater output than was possible.

Clothing, as a Wages Council industry, had its basic minimum wage rates set nationally. But each company had its own bonus system on top of their basic rate. By keeping basic wages low and the proportion of the wage determined by the machinist's performance high, management had a highly effective means of control. At least they had in theory.

Julie described what happened when her productivity was inadvertently too high. Before she had been put on the elasticator she was put on another job. She had not worked as a machinist for several years and this was to enable her to get back her skills. "I started on the Monday. By the Wednesday I was on piecework and the girl whose job it was the shop steward, wasn't she? She was off on the sick. Well, I didn't know this but she couldn't make her money on it, could she? Well, can you imagine when she came back! There was all hell let loose! She says to me, 'How many were you doing an hour?' I says, 'Forty two.' She says, 'Well, I've been doing it for six weeks and I can only do twenty.' Well, there was nearly a strike! But nobody warned me."

"I mean if that had been me and I had seen a strange person put on the job and I knew the situation, I would have said to that person, 'Watch it. Mind she can only do such and such. You'll have to do the same as her.' I mean it was a simple job. I was just rattling them off. 'Course when she came back and they took me off, the Work Study engineer was saying, 'If she could do that many, you could do it.'"

This incident illustrates how the workforce developed strategies for dealing with the strategies of management. Another example was **June's** description of how they "got crafty" and introduced extra trays to the conveyor belt in the early days of piecework systems in the clothing industry.

Wages

Angela Coyle writing in 1982 about women's pay in clothing, says, "relative earnings in the industry have declined since the 1950s. The continuation of government controls on clothing production in the early post-war period meant that in 1950 the industry could attract labour by offering rates of pay that were above the manufacturing average, but particularly since 1971 there has been a continual decline in earnings in clothing relative to manufacture as a whole." Despite this, the women I talked with relied on getting jobs in clothing, which were, throughout the period, easily available. As Julie's husband said, "It must be nice to pick and choose, like, in this day and age."

Nancy described, in 1984, how she had found a girl crying because her wage on bonus had dropped from £110 to £92. "'Ee, my God', I says, 'my husband's not even on that £110 and he works in the bottom of a ship and he had to study for six years - and all this muck and oil and being a marine engineer, a marine engineer, and he isn't guaranteed that!' This was before the last pay rise and he was on £106, I think. I thought, 'For forty hours sitting and listening to music! Daresay you were slogging, pet' but she's a nineteen-year-old bairn. And she wasn't doing, like, a collar job or a specialised job, She was just sitting sewing, just straight, you know." Twenty years before, when Nancy worked at the plywood factory, she and her father had been shocked to discover that she was earning more - £15 a week - than he was earning in the shipyard - £12.

Nancy's reaction to the nineteen-year-old brings out how

difficult it was for women in the north east to feel that their work was in any way exacting when compared with the work done by men in its traditional industries. The physical strength and endurance combined with the skills the jobs required, meant that respect for those who did such work was deeply embedded in the culture of the area. It also gave the people of the north east a dogged endurance of other kinds of privation and suffering.

Combining Work and Family

Of the women I talked with, it was the women who worked in clothing who most raised issues about how they had managed childcare and working.

June worked at Pelaw Tailoring between the births of her three daughters and two separations from her husband. When her youngest child was two, she went back and the manager said, "We'll never get rid of you, June!"

"I used to put Susan in the day nursery and because I was making a bit bonus then, they were making us pay the full amount for her as a married couple do. It wasn't worth me working 'cos of having to pay that much for having the bairn looked after. I was going to put me notice in. I was on the button-hole machine on the end of the belt and the manager says, 'Rather than see you leave, June' - He rang round a few day nurseries from 9am - 3pm to see if he could influence us getting in. But there was a waiting list. He says, 'I'd hate to lose you, June.' 'Cos I used to get me number off the end and they hadn't ever getten that quantity off before... I says, 'Well, the only thing I could do if you would allow us, I could work mornings, because,' I said, 'by the time the little 'un gets up, my mother won't have her too much around her feet till I'm home at 12.30. And the bairn won't be tied in. She'd have the afternoon where the bairn could play out.

"Well, I got that I was doing as much in half a day, because you see, if your work's piled up for you, you can rattle through it. I was making as much money... But the forewoman didn't like it and she started to be funny. So I just had an argument with her and I just walked out. I just think she resented me working half a day. She wanted me in full-time 'cos she used to keep saying, 'Have you never heard anything more from these day nurseries?'"

This is a classic account of a working mother's dilemmas:

anxious to retain the job; not let the manager down; not over-tax her mother; not restrict her child's life; to end up with money in her pocket. It is interesting that the male manager was sympathetic and the forewoman not. Presumably she was wary of precedents being set and preferential treatment being offered to one worker.

The intense competition to recruit machinists came out in Nancy's account of trying to combine motherhood and work. "Three years after I was married, [i.e. in 1969] I had two babies and a new house. Then, when Christmas came I didn't know what I was going to do. So Clay's were sending and asking. Mrs Taylor asked us if I would go back and work on a night-time for her. As soon as I got there Mrs Hodge seen us so she started. So I was torn between the two. But I had promised Joan Taylor I would do her pyjama collars for her. 'Course Anne Hodge said, 'You're not going on them. You're coming on the Marks & Spencer's thing.' So I ended up working over there on the Marks & Spencer's team again, on the twilight shift. So I was there till after the Christmas for £4." Her husband, Paul, came in from work and looked after the children. "When I think of it now: for £4 a week traipsing right down to the bottom of Norham Road. It was about 5.30 till 9.30. I was up and down that road."

Clay's were taken over by Levi's and Nancy, along with other staff, decided to leave. "Then I got fed up again not having a bit money in me pocket. So I says to Paul, 'I'm going to look for another job.' 'You know Mrs Hodge is at the shirt factory now, and she's wanting us to go down there to work, 'cos she's keeping sending word.' He says, 'No'. 'Cos he liked the Friday night out and I had to work on a Friday night then. (I think at Clay's I didn't have to work on a Friday night)."

However, Nancy and her children were out for a walk and "I thought, I'll call in at this shirt factory and have a look in that factory shop. And this woman, Freda, was doing the interviewing. I said to her 'I'm one of Mrs Hodge's girls, Anne Hodge's girls, and I hear -' She says, 'Can you start tonight?' I said, 'Ee, I was just coming to enquire what the money was.' 'Oh,' she says, 'Oh, start tonight. Anne will be thrilled 'cos you're going to work here.' And I come home and I was frightened to tell Paul. So, I got off the bus and I went to me sister-in-law's to see if she would keep the two bairns on a Friday night, so Paul could get out, 'cos I was worried. And she says, 'Oh, I think you could make him stay in.

Women working in the clothing industry at the Louise Argyle Co-operative.

It's nine o'clock finish... it's not bad.' So when he come in and I told him, he wasn't too pleased but he said, 'Oh, get yourself away.' 'Cos he knows I can't sit. You know I cannot settle. I don't like television very much and I cannot sit and read, not unless it really interests us."

Nancy describes how close were the relationships between those who worked in clothing - almost like an extended family. The pull of loyalty there conflicted with the responsibility for her family at home.

She loved the shirt factory and stayed till she was expecting another baby. Sadly, she had a miscarriage at six months. "Our Anne was 4½. I was upset because I thought 'I'm going to get them off to school and then I'm going to have this baby.' And then when I lost it, it was terrible. You know after I'd gotten used with it and that. It was still a shock because I had had no trouble with the other two."

Anne started school. "By October I was demented. So I went down to Dukes & Markus's and got a job down there. I could get the school holidays. They said, 'You can have the school holidays, no bother.' Then, when I got in and started doing the work, when the school holidays came up. 'Oh, bring your children and we'll put them in the nursery.' So odd times I did. But I didn't like that because the older children were kept separate from the little children and it seemed to me hurled into a corner. It was strange. You went in for your cuppa tea and your bait, and the kids were in the corner, like partitioned off, as though they were cattle - like sheep in a sheep pen, I should say."

"And they were shouting, 'Mam! Mam!' I seen my two bairns, you know, in that place and our Paul's little red nose and I thought, 'Ee, it's cold, where are they?' And this woman had them walking for miles and out and she was a canny enough woman and that. I thought, 'Well, you don't need money that much - your poor bairns.' And I thought, 'Ee, you're being too soft.' 'Cos they're rather clingy children, especially our Paul. Then this day the manageress come and told us that our Paul had been through this play tunnel and lifted his head and cracked his head wide open, split his head. So after that I thought, 'They're not going in the nursery no more.' He not half give himself a knock. So I thought, 'Well, that's it.'"

It might be felt that the provision of workplace nurseries would be the ideal solution to the dilemmas of working mothers. Nancy's account demonstrates why this is not always the case.

Nancy resolved her job problem by visiting the factory shop at J & J Fashions. There she met one of her old bosses. When she heard Nancy was having the school holidays off at Dukes & Markus, she suggested that Nancy should come to J & J's. "'All your friends are here.'" Nancy said, "'Well, I would love it but what about the school holidays?' She said, 'You cannot have them off. But I'd give you shorter hours, say, nine till one or half past nine till one o'clock.' So me face had never liked Dukes's. It was huge and noisy. So when I was telling me dad, he says, 'Go and work for your old boss, and I'll meet you outside the factory and take the bairns for walks and bring them back over, and that.' Well, he had just retired then. So I thought, 'Ee, well, me mam wasn't in very good health.' I thought, 'Well I could help them a little bit maybes.' She wouldn't take any money, but pay her tele licence and things like that would help her. So I did that." Several people she knew worked there already or came later. "It was nice. I enjoyed it. It was very small and family-like and friendly." Nancy was still working there when I recorded my conversation with her.

For Julie, things were easier as far as childcare was concerned:

"I've got me sister and I've got Jim's mum. I'm not sort of pushed to get anybody. I don't have to get a stranger as I would say. I wouldn't do that. If I couldn't have family to mind him, I wouldn't have anybody to mind him. I wouldn't like to think I would have to knock him from one to the other because of my job. I would sooner give the job up as have it affect him."

In practice Julie might have changed her mind. The fact that she and Nancy were able to get help from family members shows the settled nature of north east society where members of extended families lived within easy reach of one another and where the thought of entrusting a child to "a stranger" should seem unusual.

The importance of the family as a powerful institution was continually emerging in what the women said and in the attitudes they held. If their mothers had had a strong influence on their choice of job when they left school, their children had a powerful influence later on - more powerful often than their husbands.

Nancy's husband had to make the best of her determination to work. Julie's husband's views came second to considerations of benefit to their son. When Julie had to decide whether to go back to the clothing co-operative, which she had left some months before when it seemed likely to close, she explained that the other option was a job in a well established clothing firm. She decided to go to Louise Argyle: "I thought, 'Well, it's handy. It's on me way to school, coming back from school. I can pick the bairn up. I had no worries. I hadn't to depend on anybody to look after James. Everything was on hand.' I thought. And he [her husband] called us all the stupid things under the sun! He wasn't suited at all 'cos it [the Co-operative] was still... It was dodgy."

Even when childcare was not an issue, Audrey, working at Angus's, wanted to make clear that her job couldn't conflict with her role at home: "If it interfered too much at home I would stop it. I've always found that it's better to keep your home happy, even if you're hard up. If I found it was interfering too much at home - like when the men come in I have dinner on the table for quarter to five."

While the clothing Industry provided a staple of jobs for women throughout the period considered here, by the end of the 1970s clothing factory closures were an issue. In the next chapter we hear about how Louise Argyle was set up in response to this.

Photo opposite: The Louise Argyle factory in Hebburn c1982

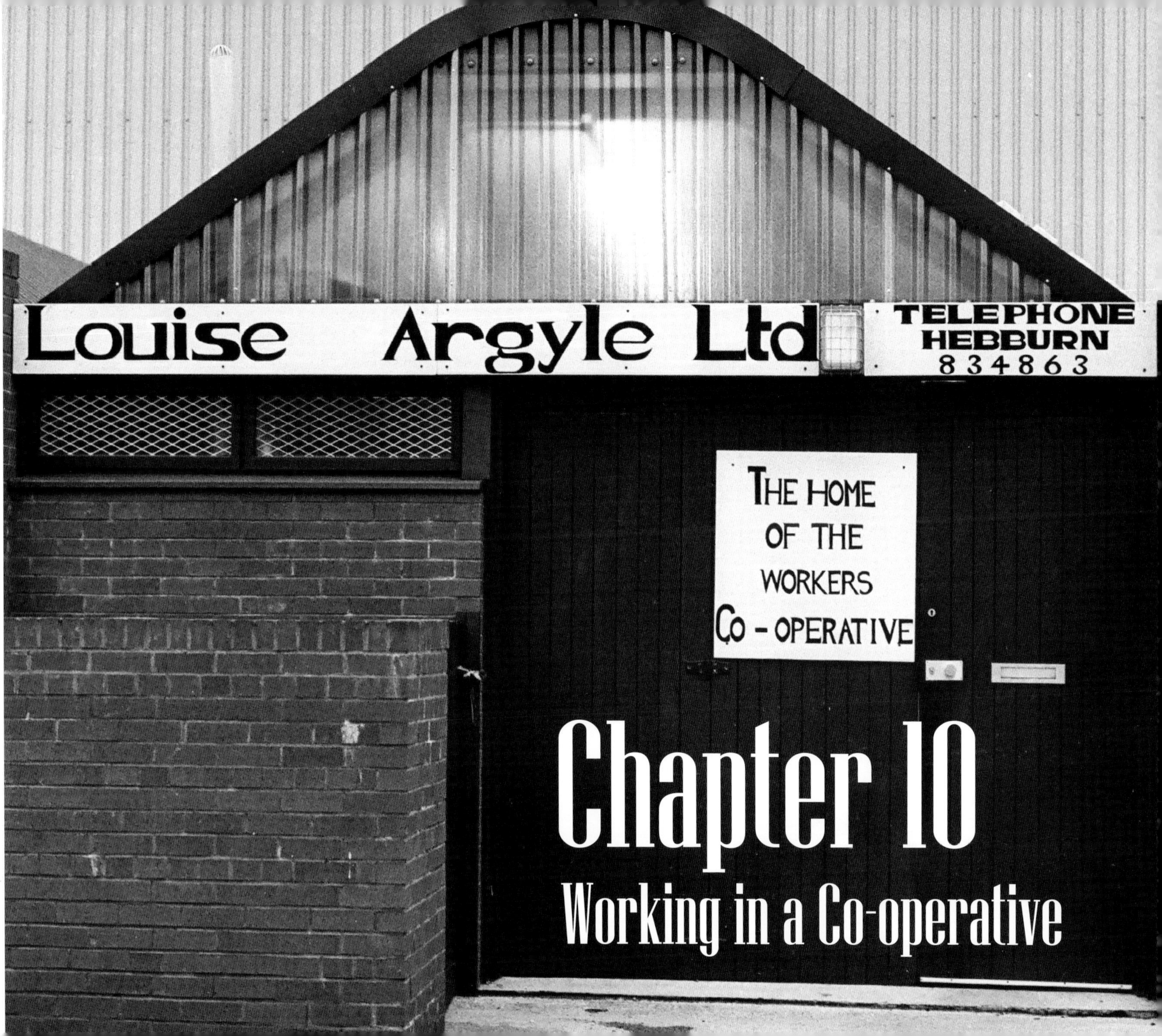

Louise Argyle Ltd
TELEPHONE
HEBBURN
834863
THE HOME
OF THE
WORKERS
CO-OPERATIVE

Chapter 10

Working in a Co-operative

Photo Credit: Martin Stott.

"When I first started at Louise Argyle, I was just dismayed. I just couldn't make head nor tail of the place. There was June and Alice and they were the bosses and Paul was there and he was the boss and I used to think, 'My God, I've never worked in a place like this before in my life.' I mean, you had the boss and the workers - not everybody was the boss! You didn't know who to speak to. I was just bewildered and I couldn't believe it." (Julie)

"We've had to learn the hard way. We've had a lot of strife, lot of heartache, lot of upset. But at the end of the day - and we're still learning and we've still got a long way to go - but at the end of the day my opinion about the co-op - it's the best thing anybody could do. For all the ups and downs, it's better working for yourselves than working for someone else." (June)

"I mean, it's not right. They should have a boss in here, definitely." (Pam)

"I think it would be hard to adapt yourself to someone telling you when to come in, when to stand up, when to sit down - when to go to the toilet and when to come out! But I think we work harder. I think we've got more incentive to work whereas when you're working for someone else, if you can skive, you'll do it." (Alice)

These thoughts of women working at Louise Argyle, a clothing co-operative in Hebburn started in 1981, reflect the mixed feelings the experience produced. It was a costly endeavour in personal relationships, physical effort, determination and in corporate responsibility. In the previous chapters we have heard about the women's experience of working in jobs where they had very little influence over the management. But in setting up Louise Argyle they found themselves taking initiatives, attracting publicity and assuming business responsibilities.

This took place against a background in which companies used the government Regional Development Grants to open clothing factories, only to close them when the statutory two-year period had elapsed. This led to a lot of resentment among those employed. It was a time of expansion and decline in the clothing industry, so Louise Argyle opened in a volatile environment.

The Sit-in which led to setting-up Louise Argyle

The original members of the co-op had worked at Shirley Kendal, a regular clothing factory. The sit-in, which began on September 23rd, 1980, was not planned. It just happened.

Just before the liquidation of Shirley Kendal was announced, the factory had been working on a £26,000 skirt order which the manager said was for his partner in London. The pressure of work had been such that the women had taken their own irons and ironing boards into work to press the skirts on overtime. With hindsight, June said, "We never got paid nor nowt for it."

To begin with the women supported the manager. But when the last group of workers, not laid off, were told that they could work for the week without being paid, Marion, one of the workers, called a meeting at her house inviting the manager and saying, "the girls were all in an upset state."

June took up the story. "So he come into the house. Now we were all sympathetic towards him, because he was telling w' the tale that this partner had sprung this on him. We were all feeling sorry for him and said we would work till he could get himself out of the mess, for no wages, for a certain length of time. He says, 'Girls, I don't want you, very kind of you, but yous only going to make matters worse.' 'Cos we were all saying we could get up a petition and we'd get this partner for you, for the dirty trick - 'cos he was making out that he had left him in the cart."

"When he went and Marion seen him to the door he says, 'I've got a few pairs of jeans if you want them.' Well, Marion started to think and when she went right up to his car, his car was loaded from the bottom to the roof with all the jeans that had been made that day in the factory!

"When we come back in, Marion says, 'I don't like the sound of this. We offered to help him and he doesn't want us. There's a rabbit off somewhere." Marion's husband suggested they should all go to the factory first thing in the morning and see what was going on. They were to meet at eight o'clock.

June continued: "I didn't expect what happened that morning. So we all meets. It was cold - a chilly morning and we got there for half past seven. So we had a walk down, round the bank to the factory. There was nobody around. Well, we stood a bit and we thought, 'Well, we're stupid.' 'Cos they have still, little tea rooms on the front. So we went back and had a cup of hot tea to warm w' up. And we come back over again. Still no signs of anybody. So one of them was dying to go to the toilet so we went round the back of the factory where there was grass, spare ground, nobody sees you, to use it as a toilet. So on w' way back - it was an act of fate - on w' way back to the front entrance, we just gets to the corner and Marion comes, [hoarse whisper] 'There's the manager and the foreman. One of the doors was open so we just opened the door, they didn't know we were there, you see. We just all walked in ... and just sat down on w' chairs. The manager was at the other end of the factory in the office. He come out and he seen w' and he says, 'What are you doing here, girls?' He was, like, trying to be pleasant. Well, Marion wasn't pleasant back to him. She says, ' We're here and we're here to stay. We're not budging,' she says, 'This is a sit-in!'

"Well, I was a bit frightened. I didn't expect - I wasn't like then what I've learned to be and what's made us like I am now. I was a bit frightened. I had never been involved in anything in all my years of working, in any dispute or aggro or anything like that, till this happened. So I says, 'Ee, well, what does that mean, Marion?' She says, 'It means -'. I says, 'Well, what about when we've got to go home?' She says, 'We don't go home tonight. We're staying here.' 'Ee,' I says, 'Are we?. We'll get wrong off the manager!' She says, 'It doesn't make any bloody difference! He'll lock w' in won't he? He'll not stay here all night. He'll have to go home. We'll just stop here.'

"I didn't want to desert them, you know. I didn't want to say, 'Oh, well, I'm not avail..' I says, 'Well, how will I get word home for the bairns, like?' I mean, I always called them "the bairns" but they were old enough to see to theirself. So anyway, I think I phoned a neighbour up. The telephone wasn't cut off you see - so we stayed there. I was choking for a cuppa tea. I never went prepared for anything like that."

Some of the others phoned friends who lived near: "'Can you bring w' a flask of tea? We're starving. We've got nowt. We're having a sit-in. Are you coming over?' Well, they all started coming with groceries and stuff and they were shoving them through the letter box and through the toilet windows and everything! Ah, but we got it organised. It was smashing!"

The first night they just sat in chairs and the manager told them the burglar alarm was on and they must keep to a restricted area. It was not clear whether this was true but by the second night a local councillor had organised bedding and told the manager there was no need for the alarm since the factory was occupied.

June continued, "So we had all the area of space. We could go to the canteen and cook hot meals if we wanted with the oven... Well, the beds and the bedding had to be handed [through the window] - and they couldn't stop them from being took through the office to bring into the factory. The people were coming in cars. There was nurses coming. Then the newspaper people started coming. Then the television cameras. And the Union was keep coming down. And then we'd get these Militant political and Workers' Revolutionary Party, the Newsline, coming and wanting to know about w' dispute. Politics was getting into it and, Oh, my God, ee! I was starting to get more aware of things, and my back up, and interested, and I felt I wanted to fight for your rights."

June was made a shop steward. "'Cos they said, 'You're a good fighter.' I don't know, something just seemed to click. I'm not a stirrer or an aggro person that would cause trouble. It's got to be for unfairness done to somebody... But I think it was because you were so full of anger at the dirty trick and how you knew when you worked for them employers you put your heart and soul into it and you sweated your eyeballs to get this £26,000 skirt order out and it was the dirty trick that had been done and how willing we were to help save his business because we liked working there."

The factory management called in the Electricity Board to cut off the supply. But Marion spotted the van and ran out and said, "'Do you know there's a dispute here? There's a sit-in here.' So the lad said, 'Oh, right pet, we won't cross your picket line' and away they go. So this got the manager's back up."

In the first week of the sit-in the women arranged with the Union to have a bus to take them to London to picket the partner's factory.

They ran a shift system on the sit-in so that they got a chance to go home for a bath and "to get away from the pressure". They suffered from bites for which a nurse gave them T.C.P. "And our eyes were all starting to go blotchy and red and sore. Oh, it took it out of w', Caroline." As the ten days the sit-in lasted went on, the number taking part dwindled. When it came to going to London, two, who had not been involved, came to sit-in.

June and the others went to London "and picketed this factory. And the police car come and luckily he was a policeman from Shields, because they won't let you loiter around in London ... so when we told him all what it was about - you see when we got there with all w' pickets and shouting, 'Come out you bum.' And there was workmen building new factories and we were telling everybody what he was. And they were supporting w' and they were banging their hammers on the corrugated iron. They were banging, supporting w', 'Come out, you bugger.'

"Well, our Mary." (June's daughter) "was working down London doing the nanny work. She got the Tube and here's me picketing and I'm standing at the gates 'cos there was a big lorry with things on going in and I was stopping it and I heard Betty shouting, 'June, June!' I says, 'He's not getting - Ee,' I says, 'Mary!' And the lorry went!"

Two of the women and the union official went in to see the partner, who took the line that a great fuss was being made unnecessarily and that other orders would have been forthcoming.

After the visit to London, the union official wanted the women to abandon the sit-in. They were unwilling to do this because they hoped to "save" the factory and reopen it. The managers succeeded in getting the electricity cut off by managers from the Electricity Board. This meant there was no heat and light except for a calor gas stove lent by workers in a neighbouring factory.

The women were determined to remain and June rang the local radio to publicise their plight, emphasising that men had cut off the electricity on a group of women. What turned out to be their last night in the factory was bitterly cold. June was worrying about the radio interview she was to do in the morning.

When the call came she was asked if they were still going to continue. "I said, 'Oh yes, no cold is going...They're not going to drive us out. When we leave here it will be because we want to go' - like nobody will force us out and this martyrdom on the phone! He said, 'I think yous are very brave women. Do you know it's been the coldest night of the year?' (All this slavver!). I says, 'Well, we've never really felt it. We're so full of aggro and passion...' I told him about the way that the rag trade is being exploited. Using ratepayers' money, getting government grants, making out that they're going to give the north east workers jobs

and what are they doing? Free rent, grant money - and then when the two years' up they pay back voluntary liquidation. Then you're thrown out on the scrapheap. Well, this time they've played with the wrong ones when they've played with Shirley Kendal's crowd.' All this slavver. That ended that and, ee, was I glad!"

June went on to describe how, after this demanding beginning to the day, the women tried to resist attempts by the management and the union to persuade them to abandon the sit-in. They were threatening to chain themselves to the machines and were preventing the liquidator from getting on with his task. By this time the women were very tired and it seems that they were only able to see their aim as being to stay put until the factory was reopened and their jobs somehow restored.

Eventually the union official persuaded them to go home, June explained, by saying, "'You cannot do no more sitting-in. You can do more on the outside. Your fight isn't over. Don't think we're deflating yous. It's just beginning. But you're tied in here. But when you get out you've got a meeting with the Leader of Tyne & Wear.'"

So they decided to move out. June's home, where there was a telephone, became the headquarters of the process that led eventually to the setting up of Louise Argyle in a small factory unit with grant-aid from Tyne & Wear. June was glad to offer her house where she was just on her own with her children: "To me it was a new lease of life. I'd found new friends." She had gone to work at Shirley Kendal's after the final separation from her husband. This had been a very traumatic time for her. The job was: "Like a new life, a new episode for us. I was only there three months and I think that's what really hurt me so much because I was just starting... I was broken hearted and it took us a long time to sort of get over him and then I got that when I was at work and talking to girls, I wasn't thinking, he wasn't on my mind as much... So it really hurt me and shocked us when I had only been there three months when it went into liquidation."

June's vivid account of the sit-in makes clear how quickly the group of women, who crept into the factory on that first morning and started the sit-in on the spur of the moment, became a group surprised by their own power and at the amount of publicity and political interest they attracted. June herself described how "something just seemed to click" for her personally as her political awareness and personal role in the affair grew. When she describes some of the rhetoric they found themselves using in response to the media and on the demonstration in London, as "slavver" and "martyrdom on the phone", this was not because she doubted the truth of what was being said or the justice of their cause. But, at least with hindsight, she showed unease about using phrases about "exploited north east workers." "wasting ratepayers money" and "no cold will drive us out". Why was this?

Perhaps it was something to do with using expressions which were ready-made and possibly offered by the press and politicians who arrived on the scene of the sit-in. I did not take this up with her so I do not know what her explanation would have been. But, throughout her account of the sit-in, there is a sense that what she was describing was like being in a play. It was as if the group of women who opened the door that morning and entered the factory which was no longer a factory, had stumbled from backstage to front stage. The lights suddenly went up and they "were on". No wonder the parts and the words felt unfamiliar.

Another element in the drama was the interplay between their ordinary lives as wives and mothers and their professional lives on stage. Alice left the stage after the second night because her first grandchild was born and that was a priority. June was distracted from her part as a picket holding up the lorry. She ran to embrace her daughter and "the lorry went".

The sit-in touched community feeling in the area. June said, "Everybody was bringing groceries for w' and it was all getting handed through the toilet window. The bread was getting flattened!" She went round the pubs and clubs collecting money to help pay for the bus to London and came back to the factory to report progress. "I had my Sunday dinner shoved through the letterbox!" They had a full-blown Sunday dinner with Yorkshire pudding and apple pie with double cream - "We didn't starve!"

One of the shipyards had a collection which raised £200 which was used to pay the phone bill while June's house was being their H.Q. On the other hand, a local Labour M.P. whom June went to see declined to give the women even verbal support. At this time (October 1980) the rise of Militant was worrying the Labour Party. This was to lead to the founding of the Social Democratic Party on March 26th, 1981. This, and the interest in the women's campaign shown by other Left groups, probably made him wary. There is a suggestion in June's account

that the Union (the Tailor & Garment Workers) was also wary of unreserved support for the sit-in.

It was left to two members of the Workers Revolutionary Party, who came to June's house, to support the women. Through them the company records of Shirley Kendal were investigated. The company had failed to pay National Insurance contributions and amounts deducted from wages for private savings had not been paid. The Fraud Squad conducted an investigation. The women, however, were not keen to see their campaign as part of some larger political struggle. June said, "We got involved in politics and we started to get frightened." What they wanted was secure jobs and they negotiated with Tyne & Wear Council for financial support.

The Setting-Up of Louise Argyle

This financial support was forthcoming. The local Co-operative Development Association, at that time a voluntary organisation with no paid workers, found someone to do a feasibility study. Geoffrey, who did the study, stayed on to help the co-op to get established. June said, "We didn't realise what we were getting into. We didn't even realise it was going to be a co-op. We just thought it was going to be a factory with a job and we thought Geoffrey was going to be our boss and he would just tell us what had to be done. The shock really hit us when we realised we had to run it ourselves eventually."

Alice, who had left the sit-in when her grandchild was born, came back into the picture at this stage: "They said that they were thinking of starting a co-op. Did I know anything about them? I thought,' Well, I have an idea what they are', you know, and how they were going to go about it. They said they were going to see a solicitor about the legal side of it and was I interested if they did happen to form one? And I said,' Oh yes'."

She was called to a meeting at which Geoffrey was present. Alice had known him as a "time and motion man." "He didn't look the part somehow. I knew he was going to be the manager. I thought, 'time and motion man? Well, maybe he's got more prospects than what I give him credit for.'"

Alice got involved "going to Newcastle, shopping around for materials and patterns and so forth." Geoffrey wanted them to work in someone's home to make up samples. Alice felt, "That's a bit much, working in someone's home." June knew someone in The Norseman, "that might let us have a room." This was arranged at £5 a week. Three of the women, including June and Alice, were chosen to be sample hands. This upset others who had been leaders of the sit-in but they were not machinists and therefore could not do anything useful at this stage.

Beds had to be cleared out of the room and chairs and tables installed. Alice's husband brought the women's own machines in his car. Alice said, "I enjoyed it. I really enjoyed those three weeks I was there. It was a laugh. It was an experience."

From there they moved to the newly-built factory unit found for them through Tyne & Wear Council. While finishing touches were being put to the building, they sat round the fire they had brought "and talked about what we could do, what we could make. Geoffrey had weird ideas, you know. He wanted all this ethnic material and we didn't know what he was talking about half the time. I thought, 'that sort of stuff doesn't sell.' Then he was going to start a knitting group and I thought 'that's not going to sell either.' We're going to have to mass-produce things for the working class really if you wanted to make money quick."

Marion, who had initiated the sit-in, was a "passer"- someone whose job was to inspect and tidy up garments at the end of the manufacturing process. Her skill was not needed to start with so she was not one of the first to be started as paid workers. This caused a row between Marion and Betty, who was to do the accounts. They had been close friends for years and this row soured the beginnings of the co-op. This was an omen of things to come. Alice commented with hindsight: "We were warned when we started the co-op that eventually they would all leave and it would be all new members. And it's happening."

Working in the Co-operative

Louise Argyle was registered as a co-op on April 27th 1981. The first eighteen months were very difficult as they tried to get established, mainly doing "cut, make & trim" for clothing wholesalers. They also explored the possibilities of selling their own products direct to local retailers. Initially, management was in Geoffrey's hands and the financial side of the business was left to him. When he left at the end of 1981, they discovered, to their surprise, that their financial situation was serious. The start-up money had been spent and income was not covering overheads.

From the spring of 1982 until September of that year, a local authority agency provided management support in the shape of Paul Cane. His role was ostensibly to give training and to help the women run their own affairs. Julie described what it was like when she went there: "The girls couldn't talk and June used to whisper to me, 'We are a co-operative, you know. We are bosses here - don't take notice of him. Take notice of us.'"

The task that Paul Cane was given was very difficult. The most pressing need was for orders. This meant that questions of how the co-operative might function, with management in the hands of the members, was felt to be secondary. At a meeting in April 1982 the members reluctantly agreed to work for £10 a week to enable Paul Cane to employ a supervisor. Edith said that her man thought she was a fool to work for nothing, but June and others were determined not to give up the struggle. At the meeting June declared that they would "work to the last gasp, till the legs are taken from under w'." They were determined, no doubt, not to appear as scroungers from Tyne & Wear.

Despite this determination several of the original members left at this point, either because they couldn't afford to stay or because they were fed up.

The hierarchical management structure continued with the supervisor identifying as "troublemakers" any members who took leading roles. June was even suspended from work by Paul Cane for "insubordination" - a ludicrous situation. It was at this time that Julie was recruited and had to have the information about the co-op passed on clandestinely in whispers by June.

Paul Cane departed, fortunately, closely followed by the advent of Skinner's. This was a well-known local company producing weatherproof jackets who showed an interest in placing a regular order to have their jackets made up by Louise Argyle.

Taking on this assignment gave the co-op a long period of stability in which they were able to pay off their debts and establish a regular pattern of working. Louise Argyle became, in effect, an outworking department of Skinner's, who delivered all the necessary materials, including thread and came to collect the finished jackets. The tasks the co-op had to perform were: to negotiate the initial price per jacket (here they were helped by

*Members of
the Louise
Argyle
Co-operative,
in Hebburn,
c1982.*

the Co-operative Development Association); to organise to meet the weekly targets; to deal with finance and the paying of wages and tax; to deal with building and equipment issues and personnel and recruitment. An administrator was appointed to help with these matters.

I started to visit the co-op regularly as an industrial chaplain from November 1981. I had been wanting an introduction since I had heard about its setting-up but because of all the interest the project attracted they were overburdened by visitors. Fortunately, I happened to meet the members with their banner on the "Back to Jarrow March" held in November 1981, held to

mark the fiftieth anniversary of the original Jarrow Crusade. Having talked to the women then, I visited them the next day and offered to give any help they needed. They needed help with making toggles for anoraks. This was a good job to do while being able to talk to Betty who was on finishing. I remember being struck on that first occasion that someone had to shout that it was lunchtime more than once before anyone responded - very different from an ordinary factory!

Betty said that some people in the co-op still viewed it as "just a job" but she felt it was more than that and that they had to work harder. She also told me that they should have had a medical at the end of the sit-in because it took so much out of them. In saying this she perhaps said more than she knew, for in December she died after a heart attack. Her funeral was conducted by a woman Methodist minister and myself, which the members felt was appropriate. They all attended and I was glad to speak about Betty's contribution to the co-op since the other minister knew nothing about this. This was a good example of how little the church is in touch with people's lives at work and how it is usually assumed that it is family, not work, relationships which it is important to affirm at funerals.

Betty's death contributed to the determination of the members to keep the co-op going partly as a tribute to the vision of those, like Betty, who had been part of the sit-in.

After that beginning, I continued to visit Louise Argyle until I moved from Tyneside in 1990. The relationship with Skinner's continued. My involvement meant that I caught at second hand the vision of the women and their determination to make it a success. The struggle was a difficult one with very painful conflicts between members. It was good to see how members who had no experience of management other than running a household (a much-underrated skill) learned to negotiate with bank managers and Skinner's and with grant-making bodies. But the problems arising from conflicts between members were the most difficult to deal with. Many arose from issues about leadership and authority.

The Members' Views on Management in the Co-op

All the members with whom I recorded conversations spoke about management in the co-op:

Alice: "At first we said we had to have a working supervisor; we couldn't afford a supervisor just to walk up and down, we had to have a working one. That supervisor did that for a while and I thought, 'This is going to work out great.' Then she got that she was sitting in the office more and more and more and that was all she wanted to do and plan things and come out and tell you what to do. So she spoiled herself. She got that little bit power and it just went to her head."

June: "I mean we know there's got to be some kind of person to look after the work and to take different parts of what's got to be done to run a place. But in the past - and we're going to try to make it that it doesn't happen in the future - but a few times in the past, when we've selected certain ones to do this role it goes to their head and they become management and employee... and that never washes in a co-op."

Alice: "In all factories, no matter how small it is, you've got to have one spokeswoman or spokesman. You can't have twenty. Everybody says we've got twenty bosses but you can't have twenty bosses jumping up when someone comes in. So you've got to appoint someone to take over and tell people what to do or see someone if they come in. So we appointed Julie to do that, but she works. She works as well on the machines and she sort of gets in touch with Skinner's. Now when Skinner's ring up they ask for Julie... and it's working up to now. She doesn't sort of go overboard. Once or twice I've thought she might have done 'cos the kids at the bottom, they got to the stage where they wouldn't speak to her because she was being a bit overpowering with them. But you can see the certain ones that come in. They've got that certain stamp about them. You can see it in Julie. Julie's so used - she's a stewardess in the club. She's so used to having people work for her in the club, she can get people to work for her here."

Julie: "There had to be somebody to deal with Skinner's because they'll only deal with one person. He won't have people running back and forwards to the phone willy-nilly. So I was voted for that: to deal with him and that was all I had to do. But you find, Caroline, as soon as anything goes wrong, they make a beeline for you."

She described some problems over making up jackets that had occurred that day: "Every minute somebody was saying, 'Julie, Julie'. By dinner time I could have screamed. I felt like running away. I thought, 'Well, yous are all supposed to be your own boss. I wish you would just think for yourselves sometime, you know, instead of trying to pass the buck.' If everything's going all right, everybody's all right. But as soon as something starts to go wrong, they want someone to blame, and you're it - and that annoys me."

Pam and Pat were not yet members of the co-op. They were among "the kids at the bottom" i.e. sitting at the other end of the small factory unit from the end where Julie, June and Alice sat. Their views on the co-op came from a different perspective. They were frustrated at not getting experience of different jobs. Pam said, "In here you get stuck to the little jobs… like we cannot really seem to do anything right. We're always doing something wrong, me and her. We feel like outsiders sometimes, you know… I mean, they don't think that they are doing anything to us, like, but you know, we feel it."

I asked if they were involved in the lunchtime meetings.

Pam: "They asked w' if we wanted to go up, like. But we'd rather sit down here."

Pat: "They put like a bit of paper up on the wall and if there's owt we want to bring up at a meeting, we just write it down. But if someone's not doing their number, anything like that, we all go up then. She [Julie] tells us all, like."

Pam: "When you talk up there, everyone looks at you and you feel as if - you know - you feel daft."

But on the more positive side, Pat said: "I like it. There can be an atmosphere sometimes. Like one minute you can be all right and the next minute…"

Pam: "You can be friendly and too friendly, can't you? You know what I mean? I mean, it's not right. They should have a boss in here, definitely."

When I recorded my conversation with June, she had recently discovered that Amy, another member, had been pressuring the young people into stepping up their work rate and even threatened that one of them would get the sack if she didn't. The young people were all considering leaving. June, whose daughter was one of them, was furious. She called an emergency meeting at 8am and told Amy that she was nothing but trouble. Amy retorted that June only liked it when she was the centre of attention. The pressuring had arisen because the co-op had begun finishing work at lunchtime on Fridays but had to achieve their production targets to do so. The young people were being asked to help out with other jobs once they had finished their quota. June said at the meeting,"We all like to be off soon but… not to this extreme.' I says, 'To pressurise the young 'uns and make them - I'm proud of them,' I says, 'They're four good kids we've got here.'"

June felt that the root of the problem was Mavis, one of the older workers, whose rate of work was slow. Pam's observation was, "I think they tend to pick on one person at a time, in here. I mean it was Mavis before and it was Meryl last week. They always seem to be onto one person at a time."

Scapegoating, or finding someone to blame, has been highlighted as a recurrent issue in what the women said. Brenda, at Angus's, identified being a scapegoat as an important part of her role as shop steward, "You know what they like? They like someone to blame." Julie, at Louise Argyle: "As soon as something starts to go wrong, they want someone to blame, and you're it - and that annoys me!" For her, the difference between a traditionally organised factory and a co-op was that in the first "you handed your fault to the boss" while in the second, "you've got nobody to hand it to there. You've got to work it out for yourself."

The pressure of keeping up production meant that, even had the members agreed to it, no training in, for example, group relations, was possible. It might be thought that the union, the Tailor & Garment Workers, in their case, might have provided some helpful support or training. Members might have benefited in the way Brenda and Jeanette benefited from the courses they went on offered by the General & Municipal Workers Union. In the case of Louise Argyle the union's involvement was limited to supporting one of the members, in a dismissal case, against the co-op. The union mindset was limited to seeing people as "employees" and "employers". In this instance it meant that the co-op was left without professional advice in a complex and emotional situation.

As the experience of Louise Argyle unfolded, I was often reminded of the biblical story of the Exodus. The children of Israel were led out of enslavement in Egypt through the vision of Moses. They journeyed towards the promised land but had to spend forty years in the wilderness on the way. The beginning of the story, when the sense of escape was strongest, was accompanied by wonderful happenings: Pharaoh was assaulted by plagues and the waters of the Red Sea parted. Then came the time when the vision of the promised land grew dim and the immediate privations of the wilderness were very pressing. The people grumbled at Moses for having ever brought them out of Egypt. He and the other leaders were left holding the vision of where they were going and why.

The exodus from being employees to being co-operators which the members of Louise Argyle made via the sit-in was not in response to the compelling vision of one person. But, as time went on, certain people became custodians of the vision while those who came later were inclined to judge the experience on its immediate merits: whether it paid a decent wage, the conditions were reasonable and whether being freed from a conventional management structure offered more advantages than disadvantages.

The two founding members with whom I recorded conversations, June and Alice, both expressed their hold on the original vision as well as their weariness with the strains of putting it into practice.

Alice said, "I wouldn't start another one, no way. I don't think June would. There's a lot of bickering. There's a lot of nasty things said. But we were told to expect that sort of thing... but now, I think, I've got so used to it that I keep thinking, 'Oh well, tomorrow is another day.'" But having said this she went on to say what I quoted at the beginning of this chapter, that she would not want to work in an ordinary factory after the experience of working in a co-op.

She went on: "I used to get panicky at first. But now I can laugh about things that I wouldn't have laughed about at the beginning... I enjoy it but... knowing what I know now, I wouldn't start another one... And yet I think the time will come when all these big factories will close down and it'll all be co-ops - everybody managing their own. I think it's a good idea really."

When I asked why she felt big factories would close, Alice replied, "Because I think there's too many strikes. I mean in a co-op you would have nothing to strike about because you'd be striking against yourself... There would be no ownership so there'd be no strikes. I think the economy would lift under those circumstances."

June said: "I think it's because of the way that we fought for it. I don't know if it goes for all of them but I know I can speak for Beryl, Alice and myself [the original members still involved at the time] - we've got a commitment to the co-op you know, and there's a lot of people that helped w' and we don't want to let them down. I mean there's many a time we could have said, 'to pot with it,' you know, but we wouldn't, I wouldn't. I feel like I helped to fight for that place and no way will I let anybody ruin it because they haven't got the same feeling for it as what I've got."

"We are the original members, but we don't make them feel that we are above them because the ones that are members now, they have as much say as what we have. But some of them really don't know exactly what a co-op is about and this is the hardest part in a co-op. When we get a full workforce that feels and knows exactly what a co-op is all about, then things'll start to get better."

Though the founding members had a particularly strong hold on the vision, those who came in later still had a commitment, even if that was at the level of ensuring their jobs. Julie described the atmosphere at the time I recorded my conversation with her: "I think it's building up now though, Caroline, the tension. We've never had it for a twelve month. We've always been so happy just doing w' work, paying w' debts, getting w' wages, paying w' bills and it suited us down to the ground, you know. Now the tension's there again, with the uncertainty, where the next work's going to come from. It's starting again. I could be wrong. It could just be the hassle of this new order." [They were making a different style of jacket for Skinner's]. "But I can feel that atmosphere and everybody's worried. They say, 'I'm not bothered', but they are. I've said it myself, 'Oh, well, if it goes, it goes'. I'll have to send that car back, mind, but that's what I work for, Caroline, things for myself. I mean I don't work because it's an absolute necessity. But, I mean, we have a holiday and I run that car and things and we couldn't do that if I didn't work. I mean, we could live and have a decent living, but we wouldn't be able to have all these other things. Where the likes of June - June's got to work - I mean she hasn't got to but it's either that or the social. It's as simple as that with June. It's not like that for me or Alice. Alice's got a man to keep her - I have. But I'm not the kind of person that could stay in the house all day."

Overall, therefore, except at times of intense crisis when all would say "to pot with it", it is probable that those who were working at Louise Argyle in 1984 would have agreed with what June said, quoted at the beginning of this chapter: "At the end of the day - and we're still learning and we've still got a long way to go - but at the end of the day, my opinion about the co-op - it's the best thing that anybody could do. For all the ups and downs it's better working for yourselves than working for someone else."

Women of the Louise Argyle Co-operative, in Hebburn, who shared their memory of the experience.

"At the end of the day, my opinion about the co-op - it's the best thing that anybody could do. For all the ups and downs it's better working for yourselves than working for someone else."

June on her feelings about Louise Argyle.

CONCLUSION

We have followed the working lives of the women from Phyllis and Vera starting work in the North Shields of the 1930s to the members of Louise Argyle running their own business in the 1980s. The women whom I talked with were all, by definition, working or recently retired. The industrial jobs they had were those which, from the outside, might have seemed of little intrinsic interest and to have been physically demanding. But it was clear from what they said that they had a deep concern for the particular jobs they did and also an involvement in the world of the workplace. This was particularly the case with those who were supervisors or shop stewards or co-op members but it was not confined to them. Those who worked in clothing were conscious of their skills as machinists. Those who worked at Angus's were probably less aware of their skills since theirs were "in-house" skills, not recognised at all outside the factory and generally taken for granted within it. They also worked alongside "skilled" men which did not help their skills to be valued.

We have heard, in what the women said, how "going to work" was important to them, not only for the money that it brought, but in many different ways. One of the important dimensions of working in a factory which I realised as an industrial chaplain was the importance of belonging to a community. Although relevant to men, it was particularly relevant to the women whom I got to know. They had fewer opportunities, because of their responsibilities at home, for belonging to groups outside the home. They found it difficult to justify doing things to meet their own needs - even having a job! Working in a factory gave the women access to many of the benefits of belonging to a community, as it were, ready-made. It enabled them to meet a complex of needs without having to justify this to themselves or to leave the home apart from going to work. In a factory they spent time with other adults, unencumbered with children. They could share concerns with them and seek advice. They were in touch with the life of the factory and the area in which it was set. They had access to all the contacts which factory life brings: people with know-how and practical skills; sources of cheap goods and services; if they wanted to have a bet they could do so without having to visit a betting-shop - which some women might hesitate to do. In a large factory they could visit the nurse about health problems without having to make an appointment with the doctor.

Of course there were disadvantages too, apart from the obvious ones of the nature of the work and the conditions in which it was done. A factory provided companionship but there was also the culture which a workplace develops. If you challenged the culture's assumptions you could acquire a reputation it was difficult to lose. Nancy, going back to work after a miscarriage about which her workmates had not heard, was greeted with, "You've never left a new baby? That's not like you." Her reputation as a good mother was clearly on the line.

The women used their experiences in the family as keys to their experience as workers: Audrey, having a row with a supervisor, thought, "I'm not taking this. I don't take this at home." Jeanette, thinking about her commitment as a shop steward, pointed to her experience as a single parent as an explanation. Women's role in the family is typically that of ensuring its survival and cohesion. It is usually women who mediate in family disputes, keep communication going between generations and with more remote family members. They bring this experience into the workplace taking important roles in building community: providing food for workplace celebrations; visiting those on the sick or who are bereaved. June told of how the women decorated "the belt" at Pelaw for Christmas; Brenda organised the Saturday night bus trips.

The downside of all this was that the factory was a closed community. You only belonged by working there - although you could keep in touch with individuals outside work. Margaret described how she felt totally insecure when she took voluntary redundancy after thirty years of working at Angus's.

But what has been described in this book is a celebration of an industrial life that was already passing, if not "a way of life that went" in Audrey's words. The years from 1945 - 1980 were, in some respects, a golden age for employment opportunities for women in the north east. Before 1939 openings were few and after 1980 were contracting. In the period between, jobs were easy to come by. You could move if you were unhappy or drop out of employment for a time to look after children or elderly relatives.

But what has also been clear from what is described here is how little the inherent abilities of the women were developed, either through their schooling or through later opportunities for training and education. Only the older workers - Vera, Phyllis and Margaret, who had learned skills during the war, - had roles even as first-line supervisors. Jeanette and Brenda found some opportunity through their experience as shop stewards and through training offered by the union. The women of Louise Argyle "had to learn the hard way", as June put it.

This book was written as a tribute to the women who shared their experience of being workers with me and "spoke as they found". It records a period of history in women's working lives on Tyneside that could easily have been overlooked and forgotten.

Bibliography

Brown, R and Brennen, P (1970) 'Social Relations and Social Perspectives among Shipbuilding Workers' in 'Sociology' Vol. 4 1970. Part 1 pp 71-84.

Coyle, A (1982) 'Sex and Skill in the Organisation of the Clothing Industry' in J. West (ed.) 'Work, Women and the Labour Market' London, Routledge and Kegan Paul.

Griffin, C (1985) 'Typical Girls? Young Women from School to the Job Market'. London, Routledge and Kegan Paul.

Roberts, K (1971) 'From School to Work - A Study of the Youth Employment Service'. Newton Abbot, David and Charles.

Ward, H and Wild, J (2021) 'Edgewise? Experiences of some Anglican Laywomen'. London, Darton-Longman & Todd.

Weil, S (1971) 'Waiting on God' translated by E. Crawford, London, Routledge and Kegan Paul. Quotation here from Fontana Books Edition (1971)

Williamson, B (1982) 'Class, Culture and Community: a Biographical Study of Social Change in Mining', London, Routledge and Kegan Paul.